AF292446

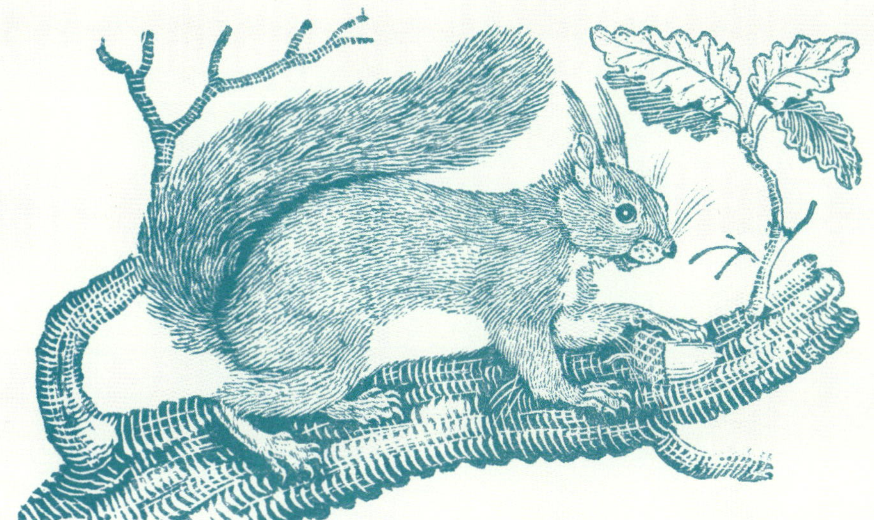

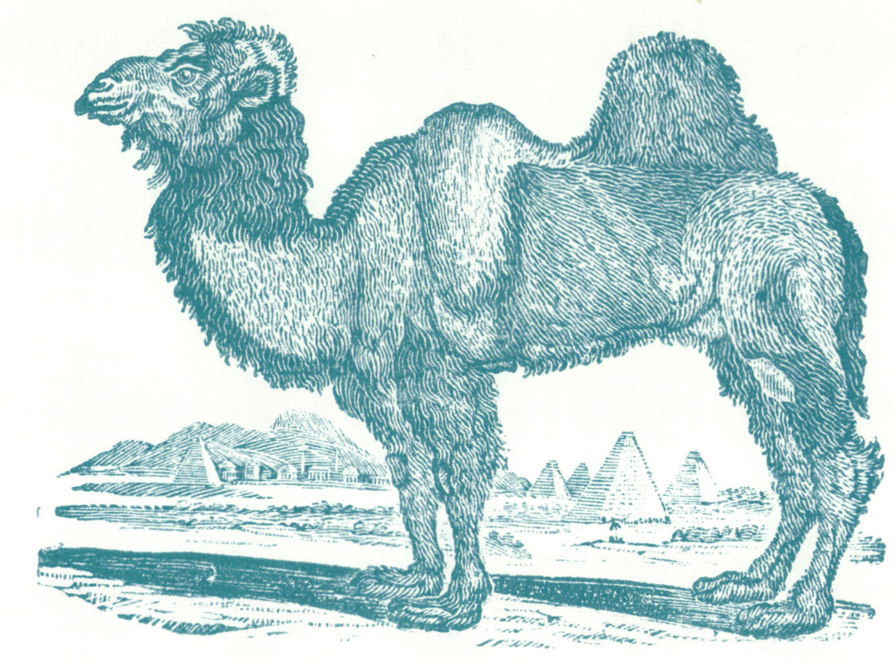

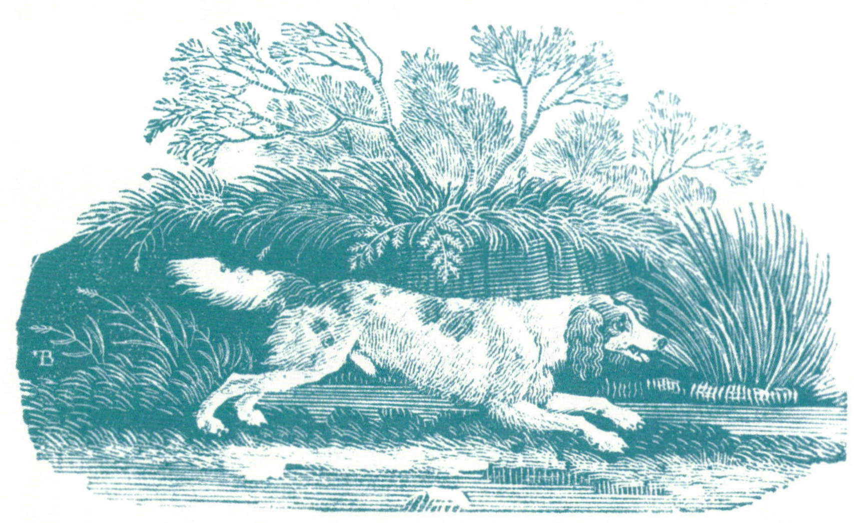

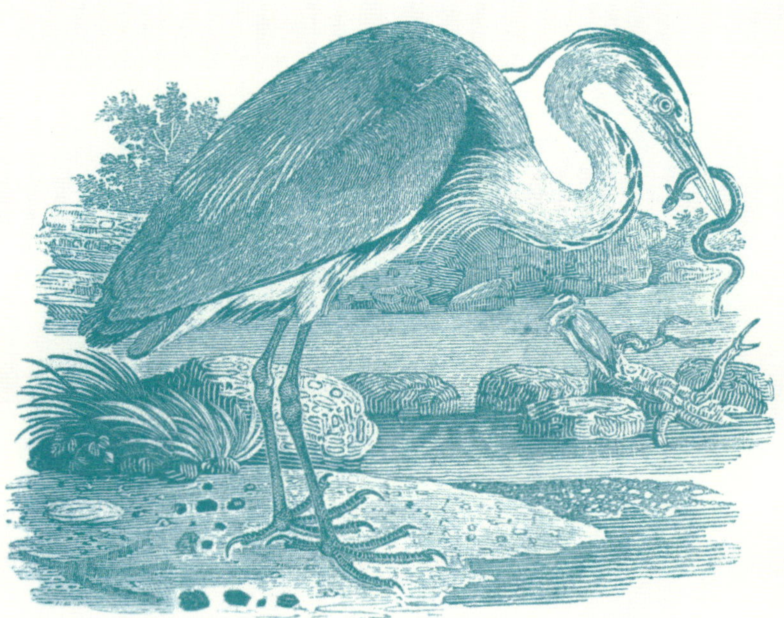

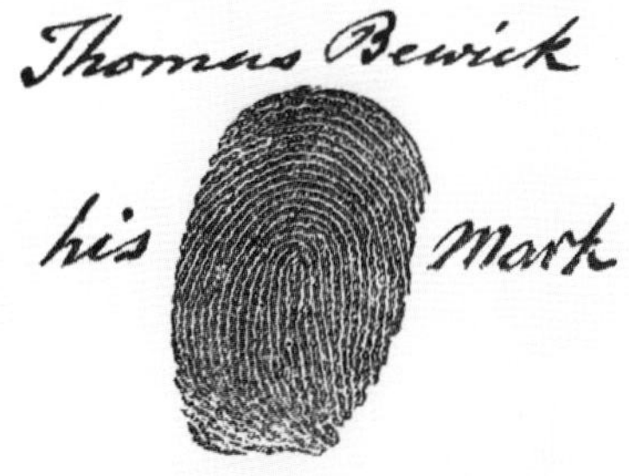

Bewick Tales

Stories from the life and work of Thomas Bewick

Sarah Lawrance

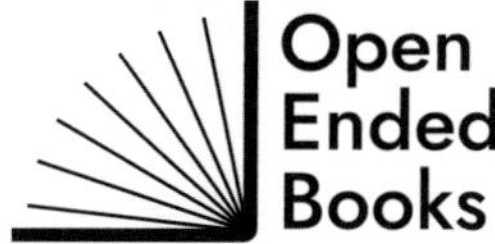

Foreword

Thomas Bewick's art has long attracted admirers from far and wide. In his own lifetime (1753–1828) he was already recognised as an important illustrator and best-selling author.

Bewick's engraving workshop provided the illustrations and lettering demanded by the commercial world of Newcastle: billheads, tickets, adverts, engraved silver. His *Memoir* provides pen portraits of many contemporaries. He lived in a fascinating period of history and change and had challenging views on all that he saw around him.

Bewick's self-published books made an important contribution to the study of British birds and wildlife, with illustrations that have rarely been surpassed. His 'tale-pieces' are full of stories of life in rural England, but they are so much more than that. These tiny images can be chilling, surreal, comic and puzzling. As Charlotte Bronte's heroine Jane Eyre said: 'With Bewick on my knee, I was then happy.'

Welcome to the world of Thomas Bewick.

Dr Peter Quinn
Chair, The Bewick Society

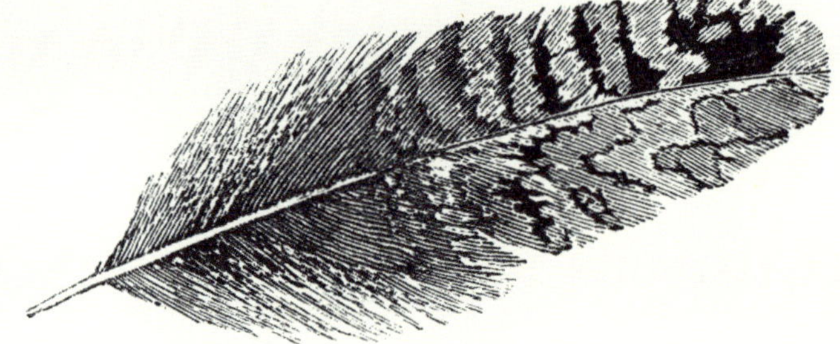

Meet Thomas Bewick

The man in the oil painting is Thomas Bewick, artist, engraver and natural historian. He lived and worked in the North East of England from 1753 to 1828.

Thomas Bewick has stories to tell, as you might guess from the books on the table behind him.

In his right hand he holds an engraving tool: a symbol of the work for which he has become renowned.

The dog in the painting is not interested in art or books – he looks as if he's ready for a walk.

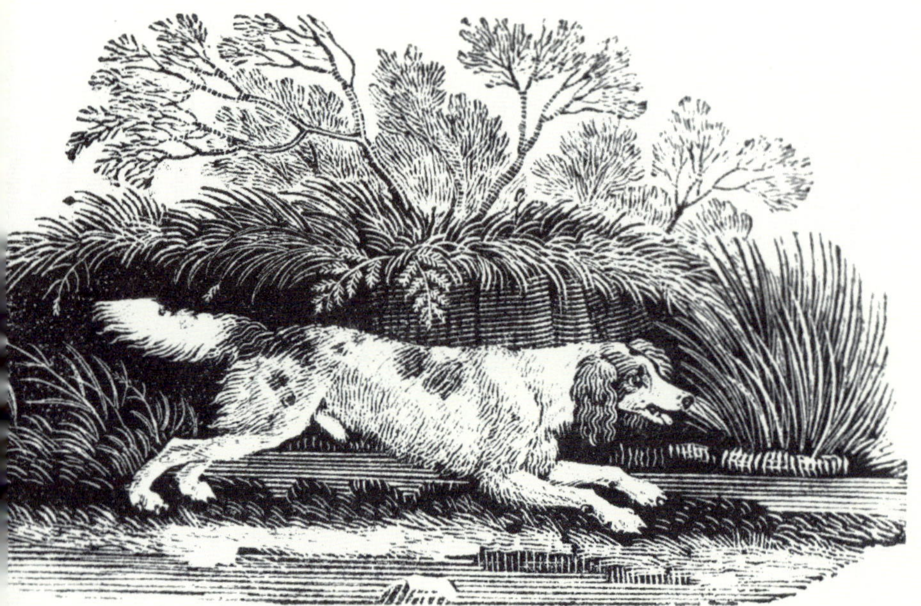

Thomas Bewick's illustration of a springer or cocker spaniel, from *A General History of Quadrupeds*, 1790

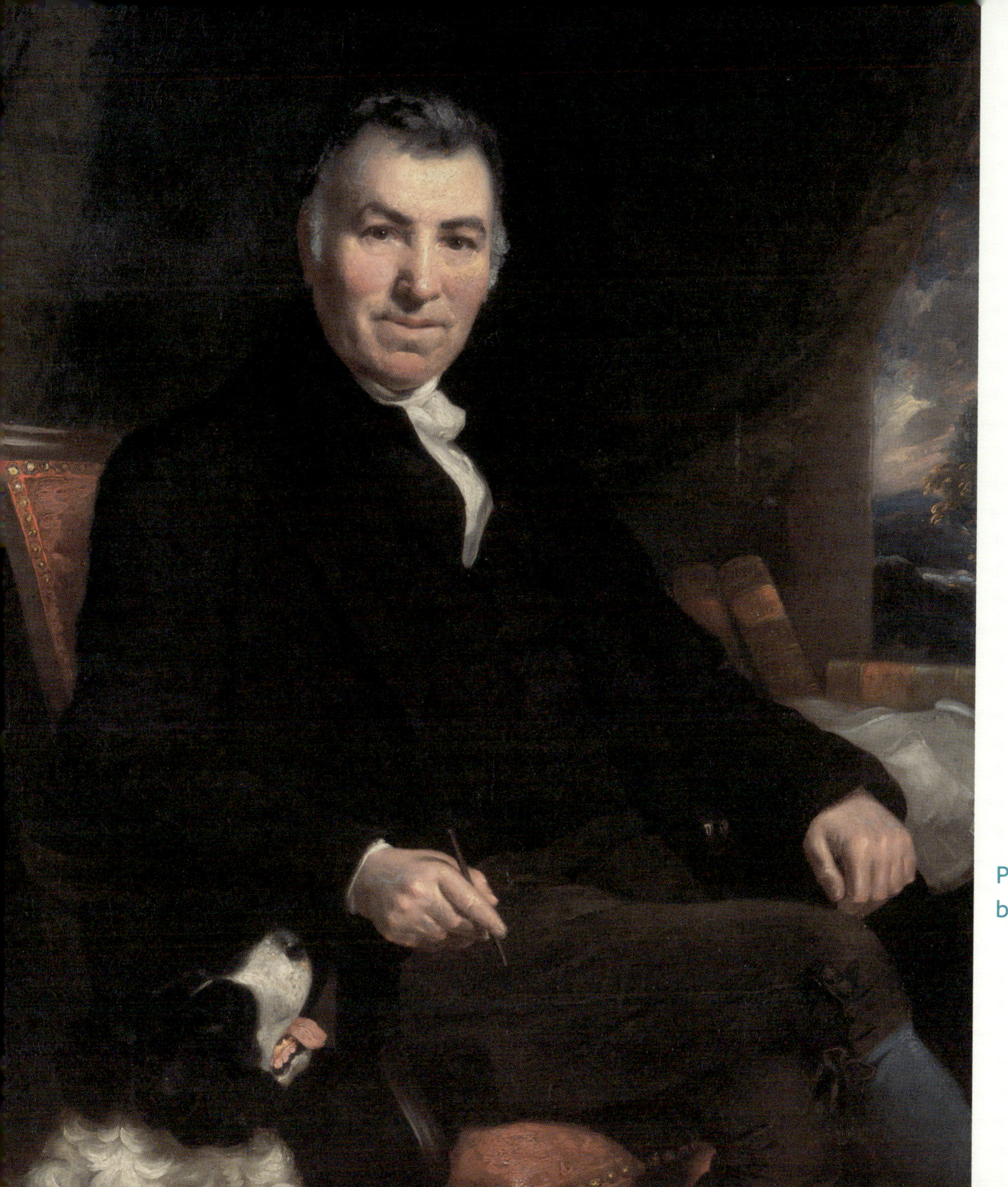

Portrait of Thomas Bewick
by William Nicholson, 1814

Cherryburn

Here, in this low, stone-built house with its thatched roof and smoking chimney, Thomas Bewick was born in August 1753.

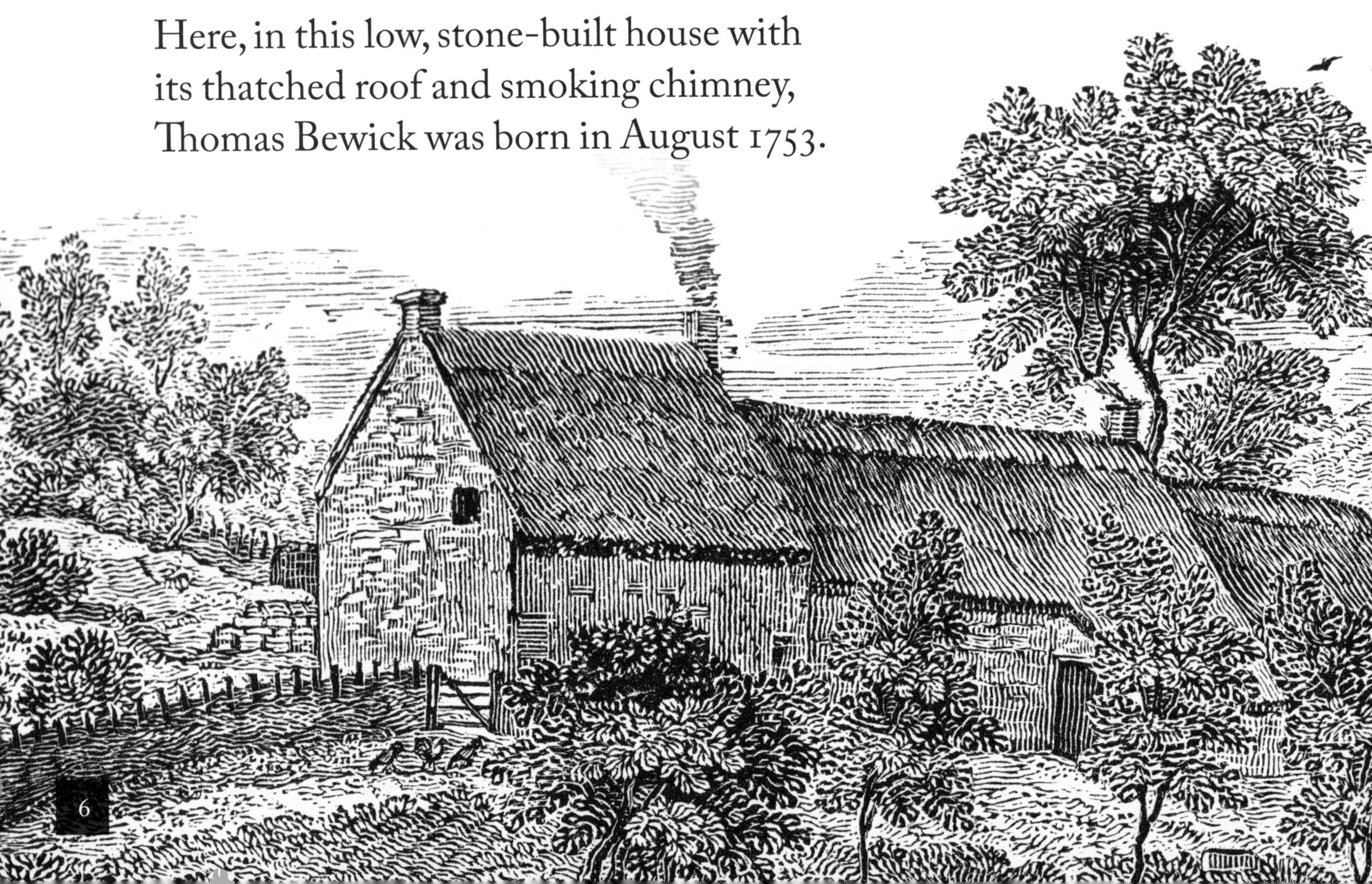

The house is in a tiny place called Cherryburn, near the village of Mickley in Northumberland.

Cherryburn is a short distance from the River Tyne, surrounded by trees and fields. The little square window in the gable end was Thomas's bedroom. Here he lay awake listening to the wind and weather, to the rushing water in the river, and to birdsong in spring.

In his *Memoir*, Thomas Bewick wrote:

'From the little Window at my bed-head I noticed all the varying seasons of the year, and when the Spring put in, I felt charmed with the music of Birds, which strained their little throats to proclaim it.'

This picture of Cherryburn, birthplace of Thomas Bewick, was drawn and engraved by his brother John.

Family life

Thomas was the eldest child of John and Jane Bewick. They made a comfortable living from farming and small-scale coal mining, but were far from wealthy.

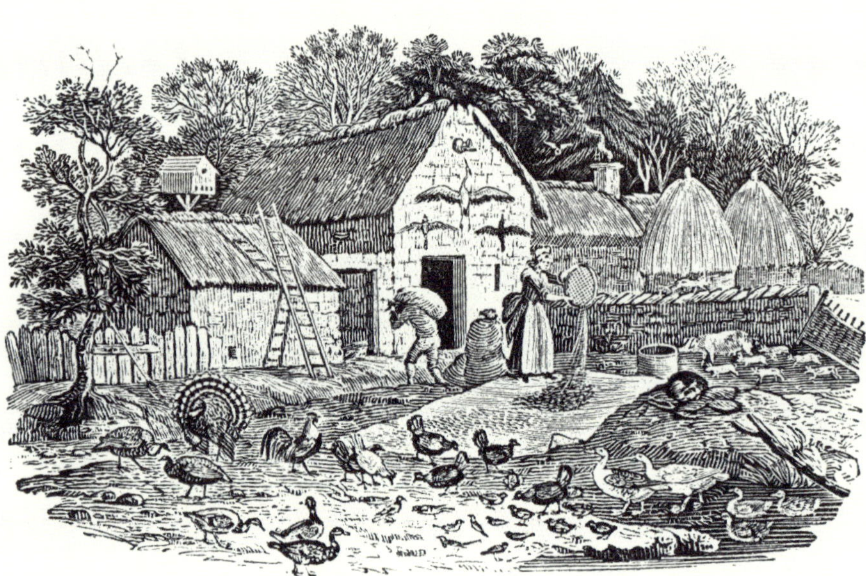

Young Thomas was wild and wilful, roaming the woods, fields and streams surrounding his home. He spent many hours watching birds and animals and learning their habits.

Thomas helped on the farm and attended the village school, but only some of the time; he was a regular truant. Yet he was always drawing, anywhere and everywhere. When he ran out of paper, he drew on the walls, the floor and the hearth.

In his *Memoir*, Thomas wrote:

'Many of my evenings at home were spent in filling the flags of the Floor & the hearth stone with my chalky designs.'

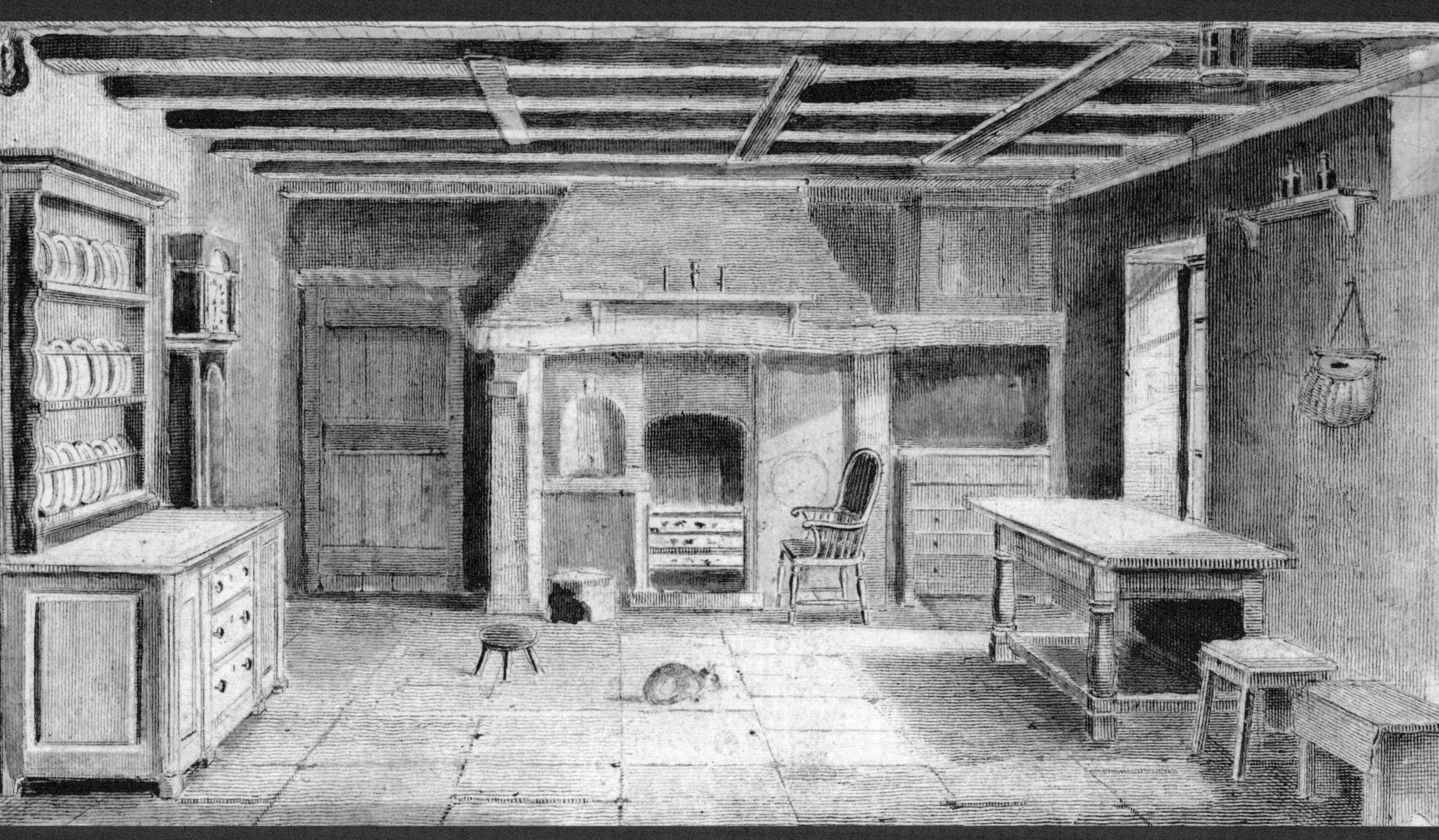

This is a view of the interior at Cherryburn, Thomas Bewick's childhood home.
The picture was drawn in ink and pencil by his son Robert in 1844. At first glance
the room appears empty, but what's that in the middle of the floor?

Messing about by the river

Thomas Bewick grew up close to the River Tyne and spent many hours in and around the water. He loved fishing, often rising early and staying out late into the evening. His father used to whistle loudly to call him home.

The lad in this picture could be young Thomas himself, or perhaps one of his friends.

Will he manage to disentangle his rod and catch hold of the fish?

Will that dead branch hold his weight for long enough?

Will he be home and dry in time for tea?

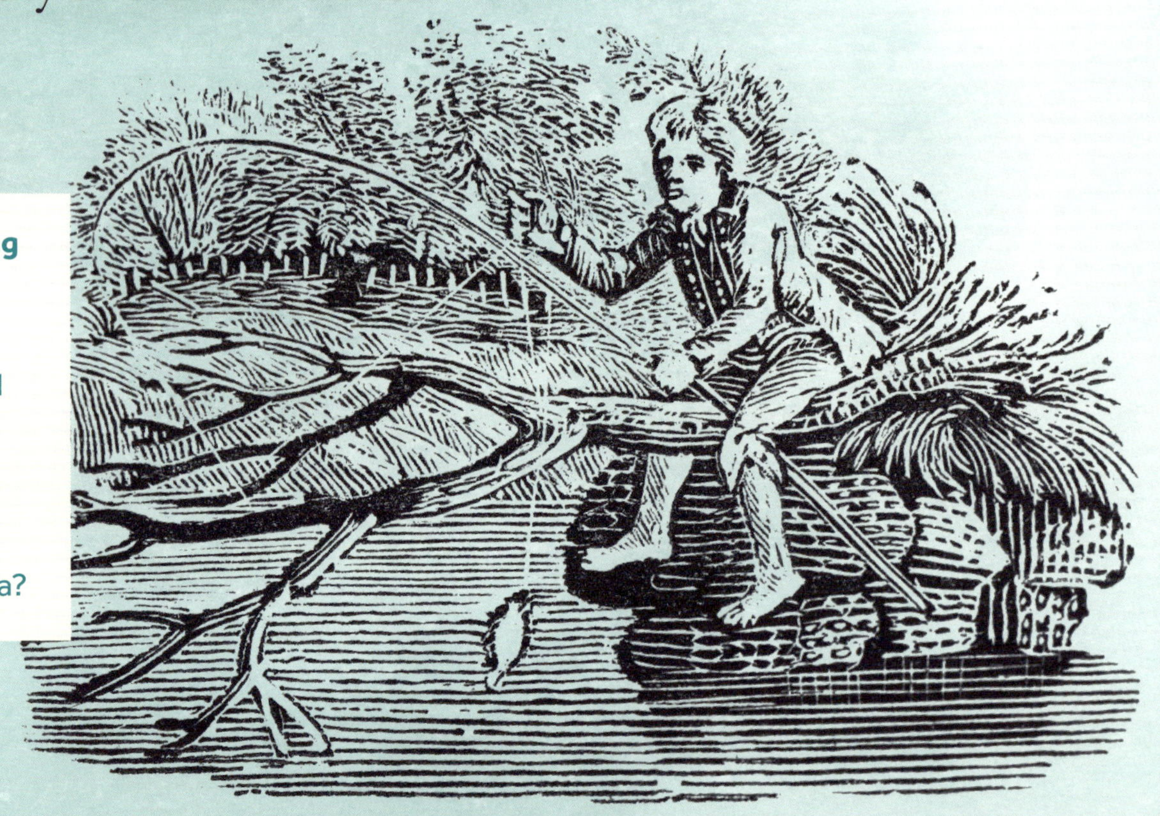

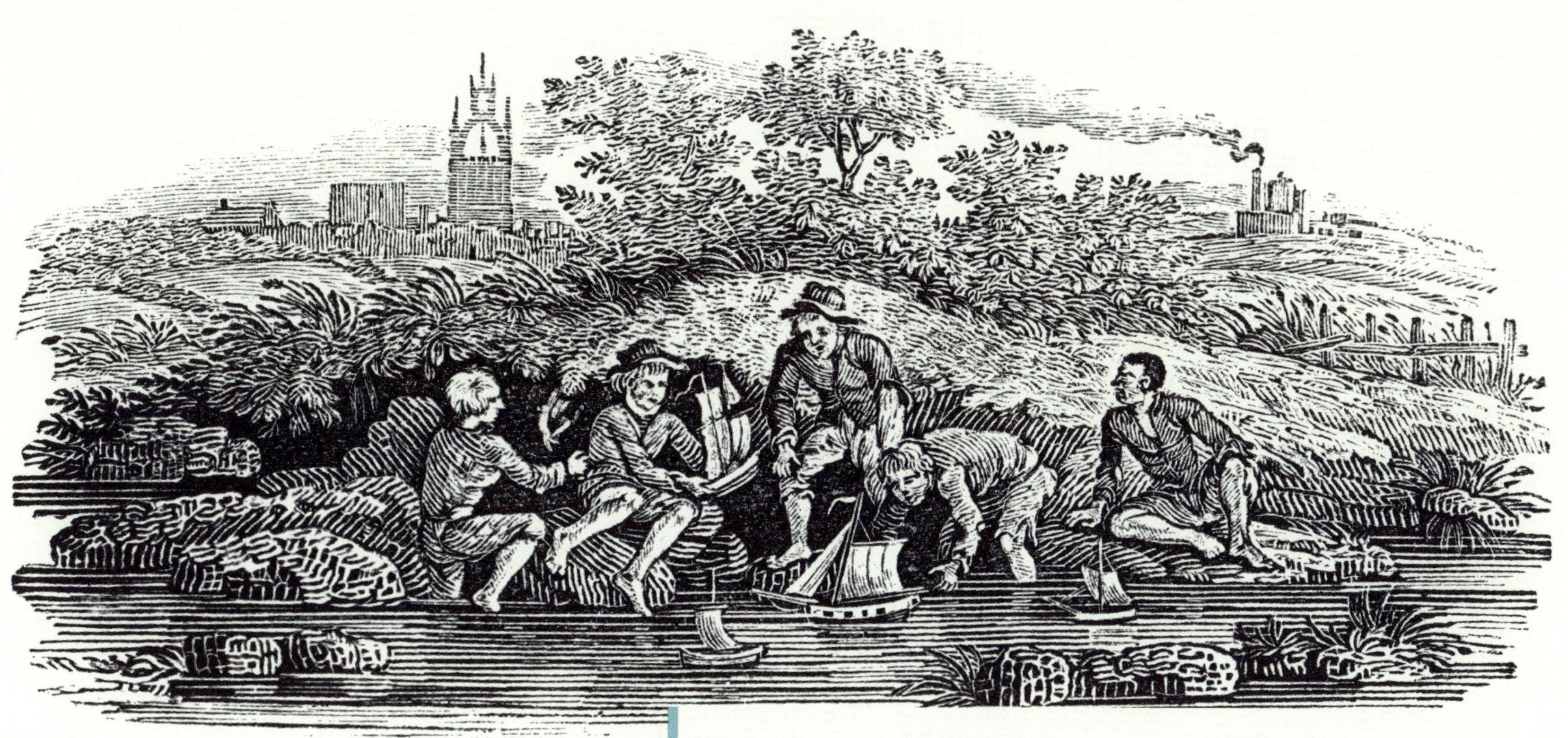

Thomas Bewick's illustration of boys playing with boats may represent a childhood memory.

What are these boys saying to one another?

Are they boasting of their prowess with toy boats?

Do they dream of sailing away down river and out to sea?

Will they grow up and work in the town, like Thomas Bewick?

Where are their sisters?

Learning a trade

At 14 years of age Thomas Bewick was a fine, strapping lad. It was time for him to leave home and learn a trade, to make use of his talent for drawing. So Thomas was apprenticed to Mr Ralph Beilby, artist and engraver.

Thomas began a new life, 12 miles from home in the bustling town of Newcastle.

His master taught him to work with silver and gold, copper, brass and wood.

Thomas learned how to engrave names on cutlery and walking sticks, and mottoes on rings. Later he was able to engrave printing plates for certificates and bank notes.

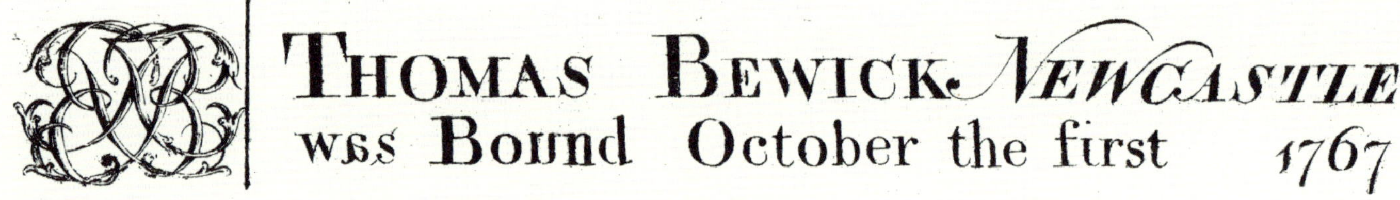

Thomas Bewick probably made this engraving soon after he became an apprentice. On the bottom line, the letters 'a' and 'u' are reversed because he was still learning to draw back to front on the printing plate.

This picture shows a list of engraving jobs completed by the workshop in the week 9–16 November 1767, a month after Ralph Beilby took on Thomas Bewick as an apprentice.

In his *Memoir*, Thomas wrote:

'Every job, coarse or fine, I did as well as I could, cheerfully.'

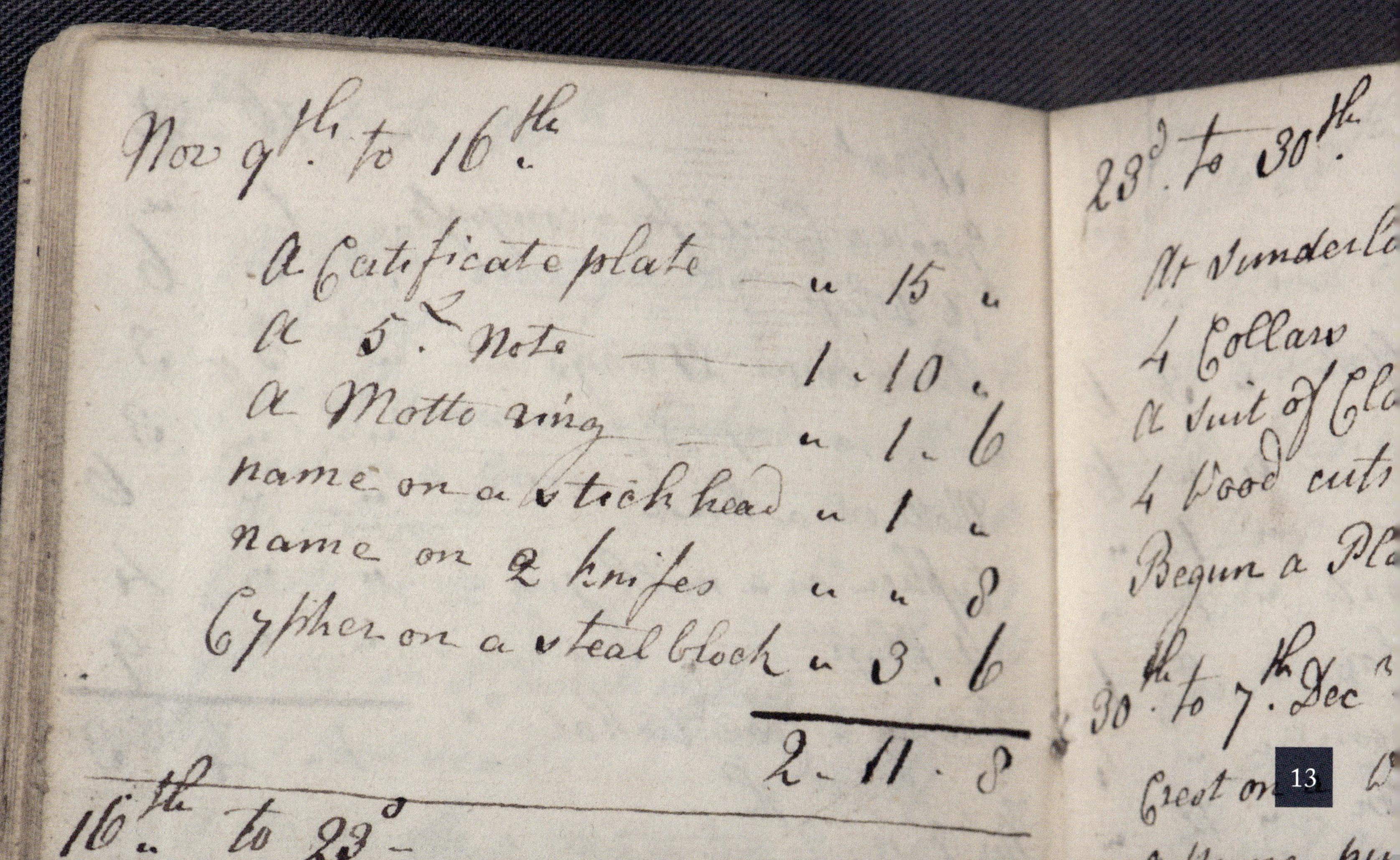

The art of wood engraving

Young Thomas Bewick excelled at wood engraving. He became so accomplished that even today he is considered to be one of the finest illustrators of all time.

Traditional engravers still employ the same materials and techniques that Thomas Bewick used, 200 years ago.

1 The blocks used for wood engraving are cut from a log of hard, fine-grained wood. Boxwood is often used, because it is very durable. The surface of the block is sanded until it is silky smooth.

2 The engraver draws a design onto the surface of the block with a pencil, then uses very fine, sharp tools to cut along the lines.

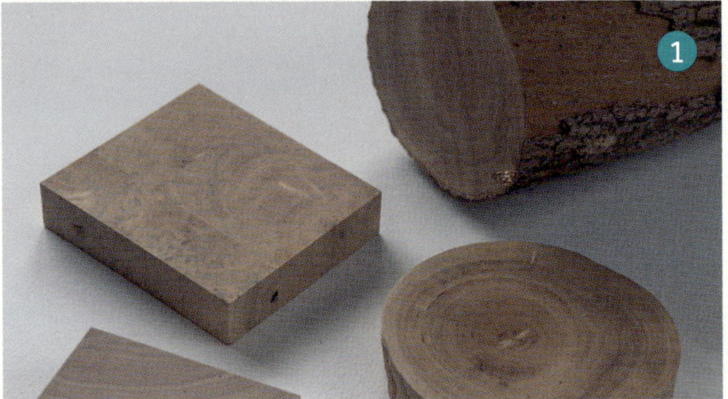

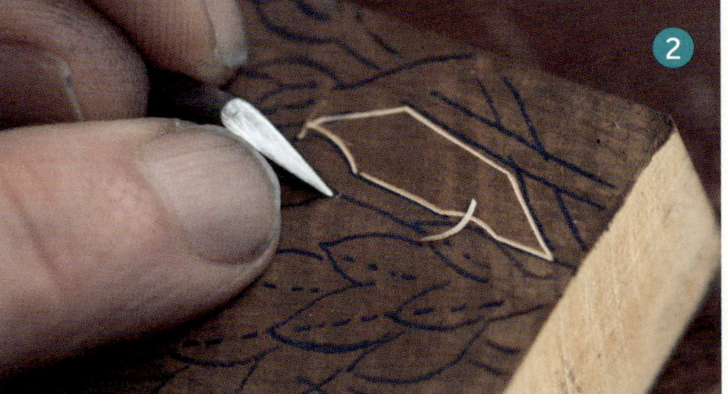

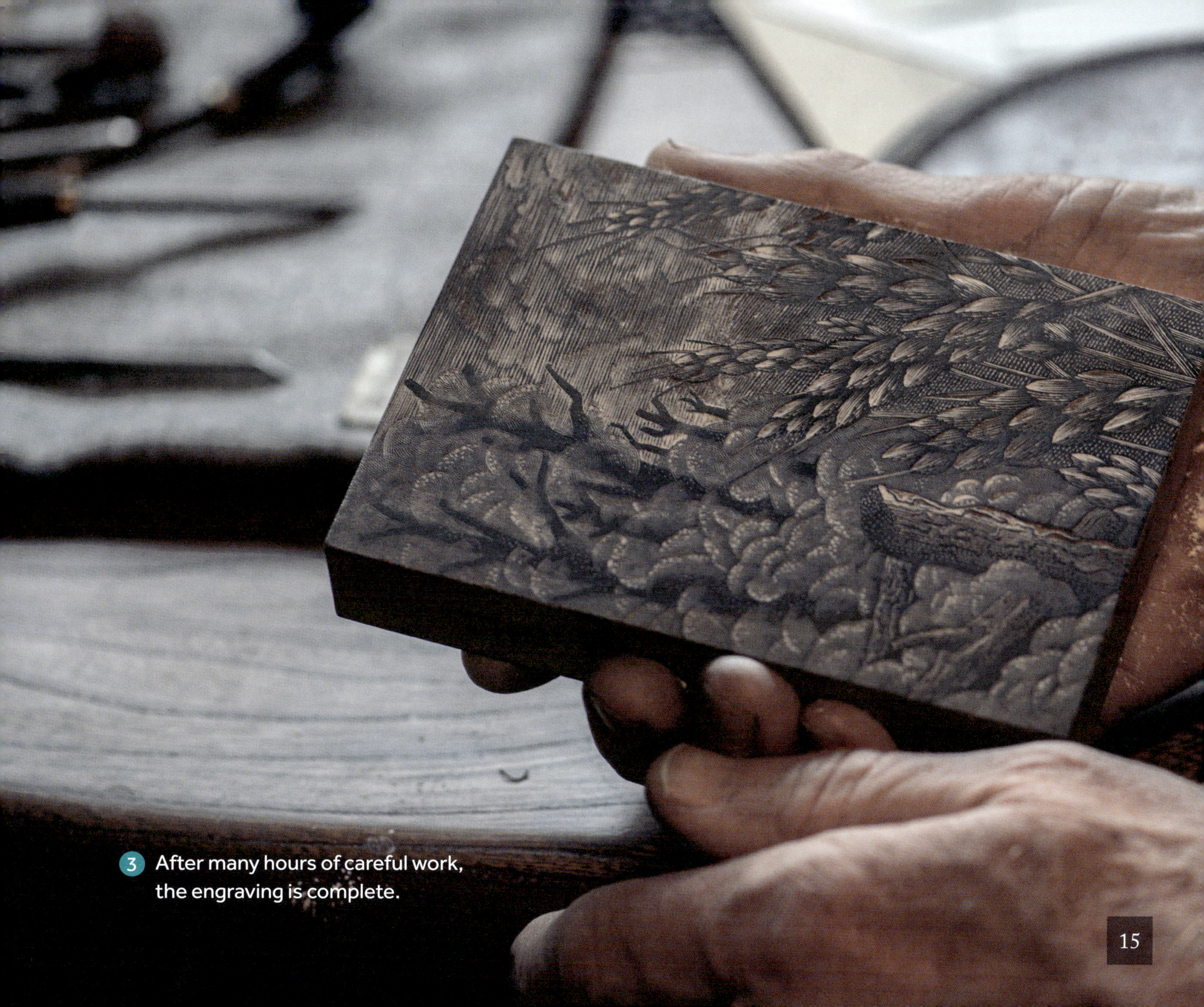

After many hours of careful work,
the engraving is complete.

Tools of the trade

Thomas Bewick's master Mr Beilby taught him to make and sharpen his own tools. He kept them neatly lined up in a wooden box, sharp and shiny, ready for work.

Each tool made a different type of mark and had its own special name.

There was a **scorper** for clearing large areas of the wood block, and a **tint tool** for cutting fine straight lines. The **spitsticker** was for curves, and the **graver** for lines that swell from fine to broad.

These tools belong to an engraver who lives and works on Tyneside today, but they are exactly the same as those used by Thomas Bewick.

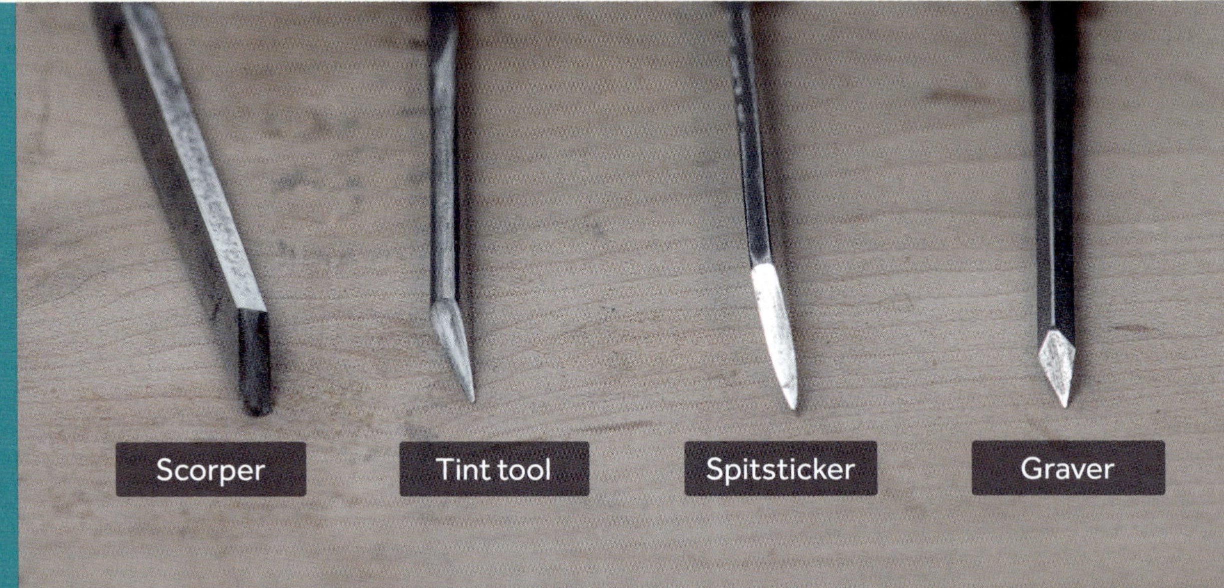

16

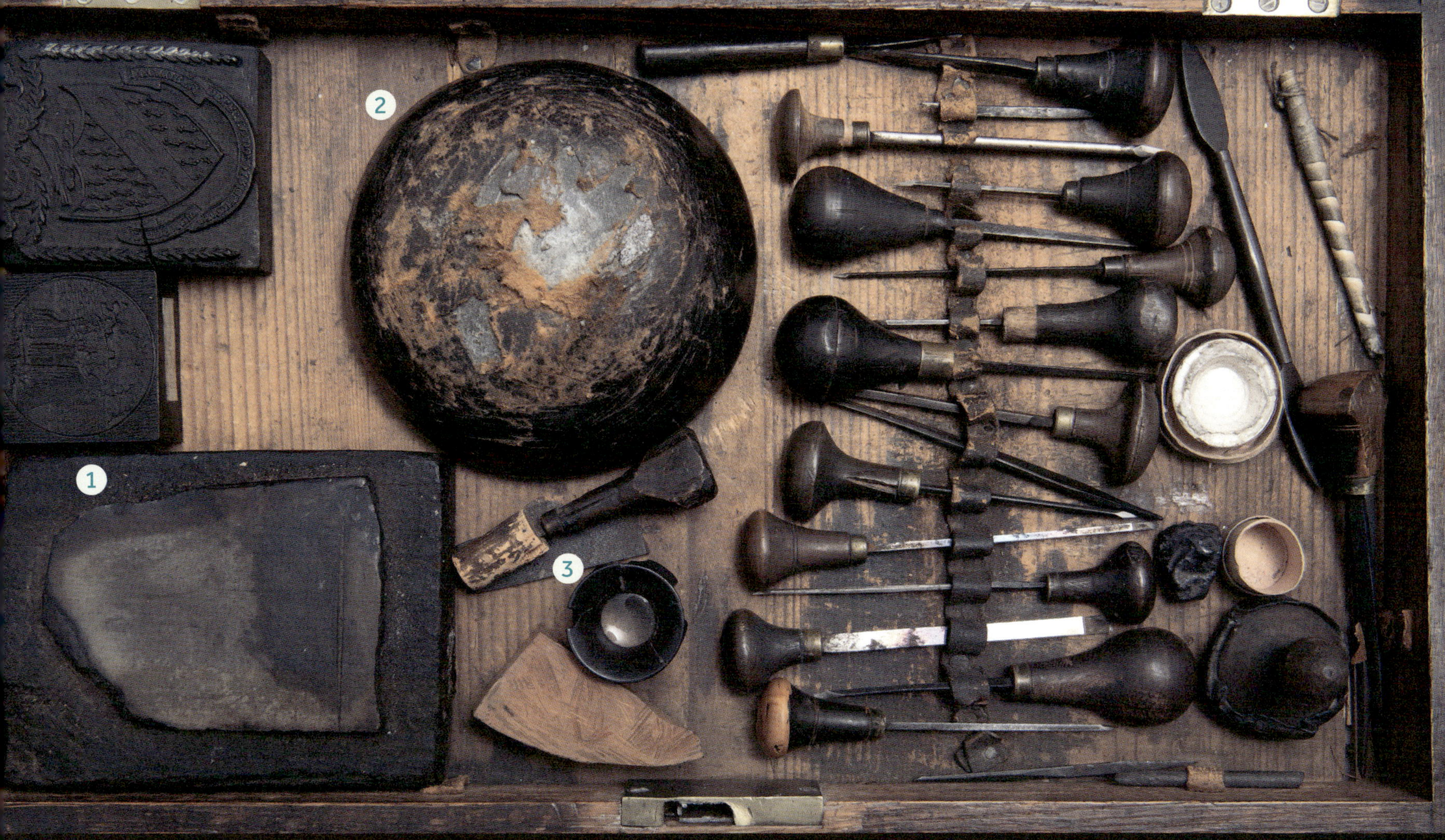

This is a photograph of Thomas Bewick's toolbox, just as he left it. In addition to the engraving tools, the box contains other items that he used during the engraving process.

1. This dark rectangle is a sharpening stone.

2. The large round object is a leather covered block support, on which Bewick rested the wood block while he was engraving.

3. This is a powerful eyeglass, which must have been helpful when Bewick was working on his miniature pictures.

Printing the image

When Thomas Bewick had finished engraving an image, the block was ready for printing.

These pictures show an artist making a print from an engraved block, in exactly the same way as in Bewick's day.

1 First, he uses a roller to apply stiff black ink to the surface of the block.

2 Then he places a sheet of dampened paper on top of the block and pulls a lever to slide the block into the press. The heavy weight of the printing press transfers the ink to the paper.

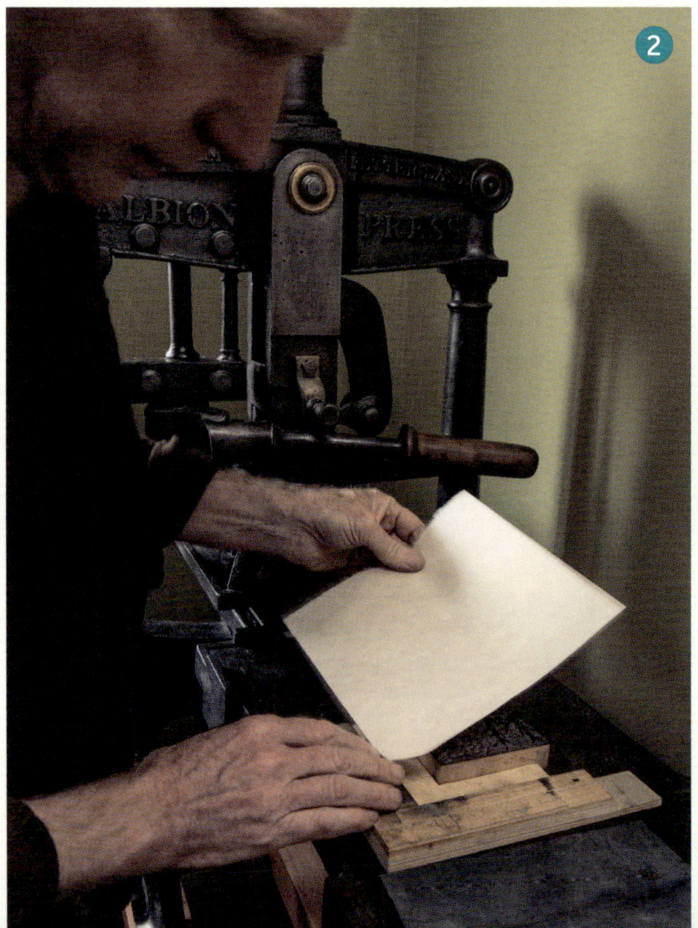

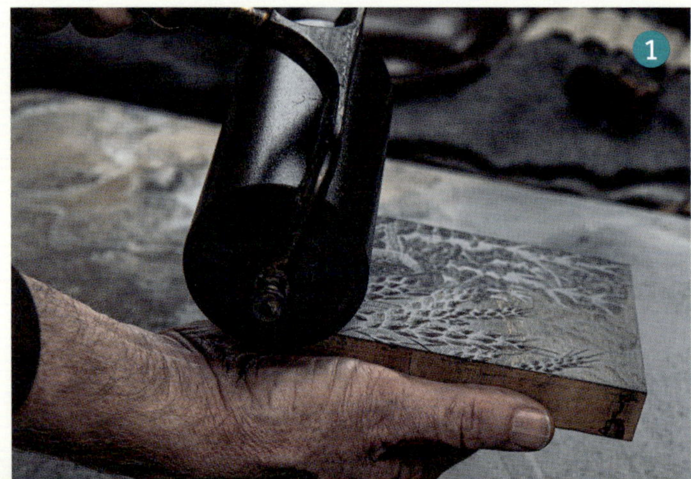

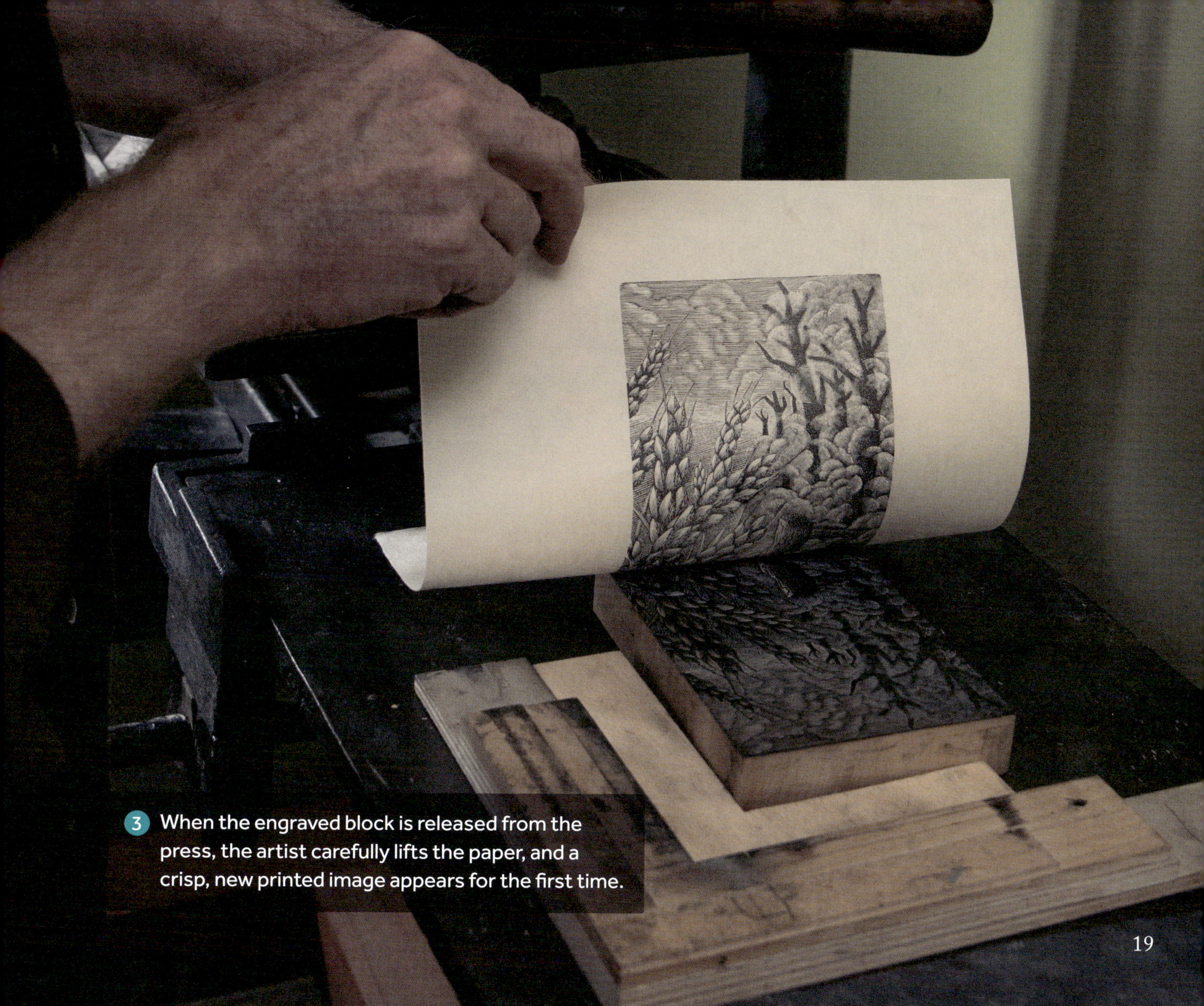

3 When the engraved block is released from the press, the artist carefully lifts the paper, and a crisp, new printed image appears for the first time.

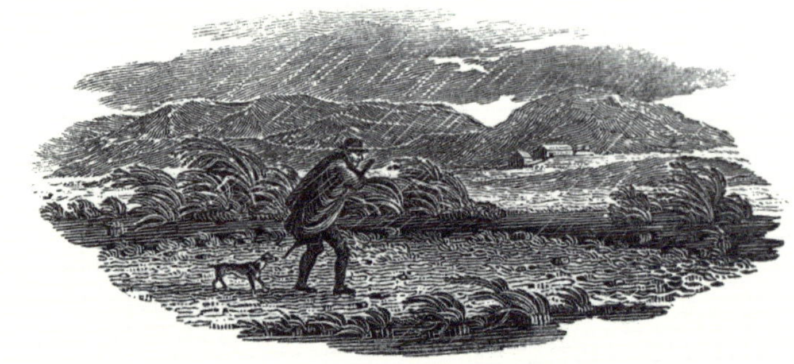

Walking home

Every weekend Thomas Bewick went home, to see his family. He walked 12 miles along the River Tyne, from Newcastle to Cherryburn. Then back again to start another week's work.

Long walks became a habit. Thomas Bewick travelled many miles on foot, at all times of year and in all weathers. Sometimes he set out not even knowing where he would end up.

He walked through wind, rain and snow. On hot days he might stop for a rest under a tree or take a cooling drink of spring water.

It's not surprising that Bewick's books contain so many pictures of people walking.

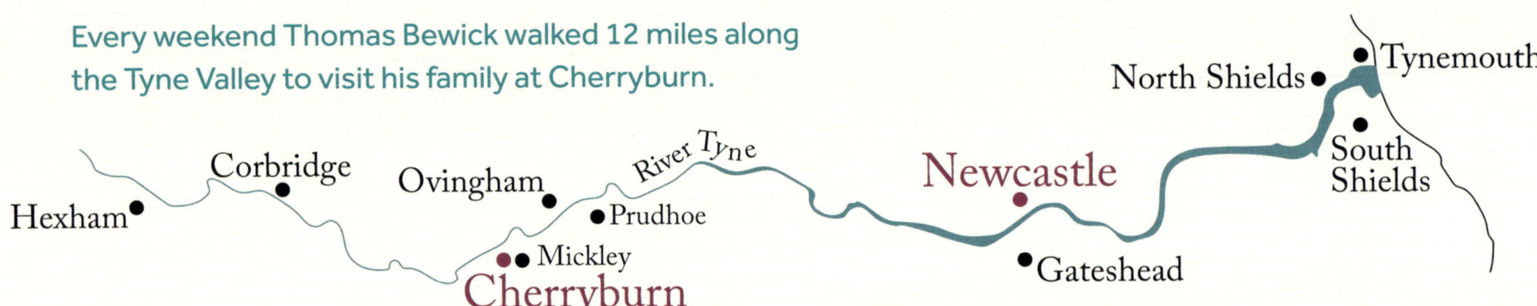

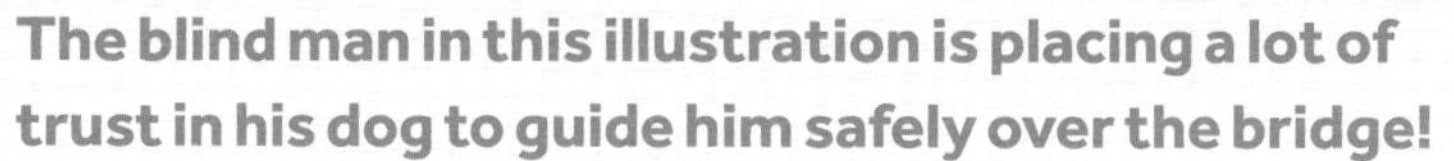

The blind man in this illustration is placing a lot of trust in his dog to guide him safely over the bridge!

Where is he going and why is he out walking in this awful weather?

Will he ever get his hat back?

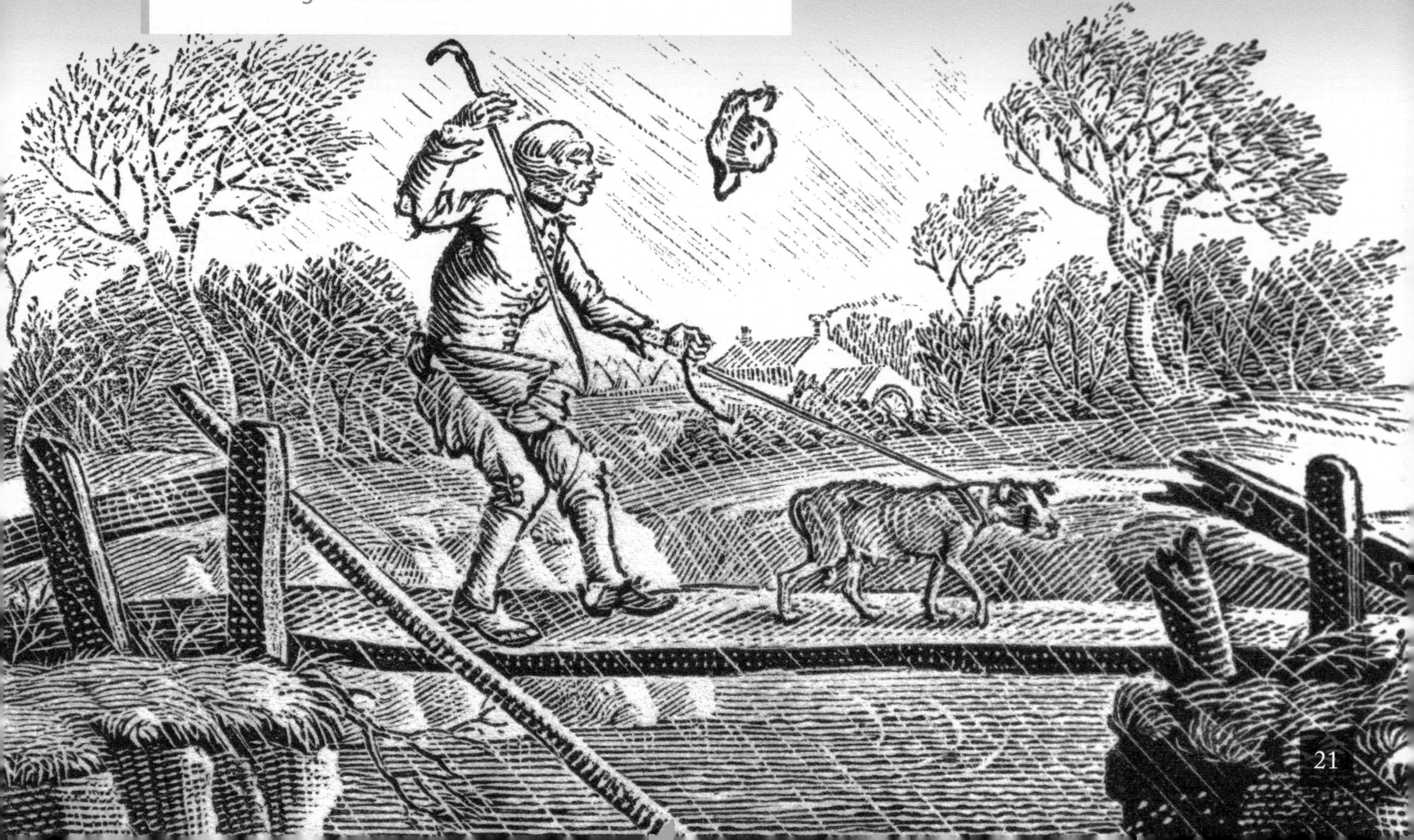

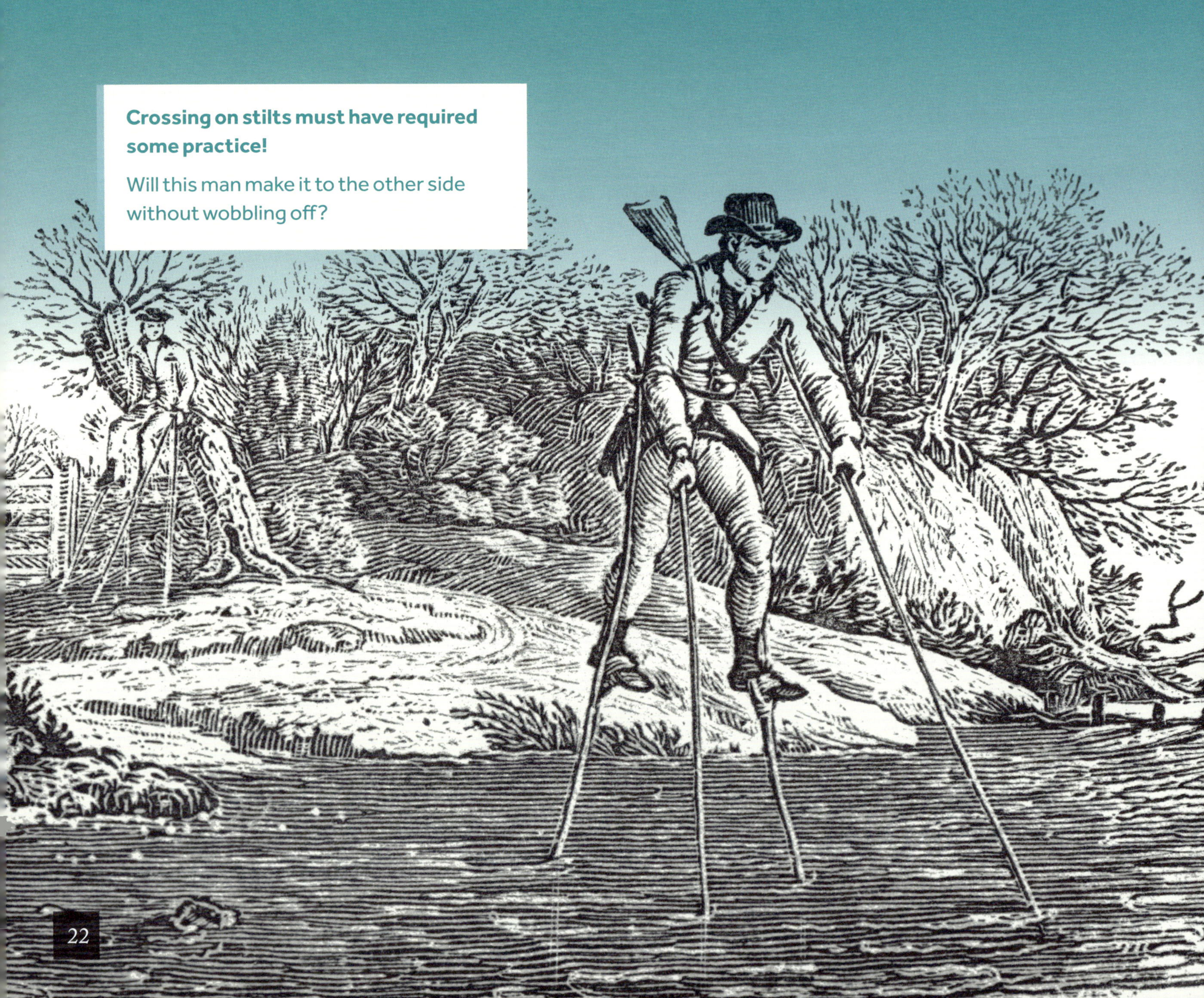

Crossing on stilts must have required some practice!

Will this man make it to the other side without wobbling off?

Crossing the river

Thomas Bewick's weekly journey from Newcastle to Cherryburn involved crossing the River Tyne, usually by bridge or rowing boat. His pictures often show people crossing the river in more unusual ways.

This fellow is taking a chance on an old branch that looks half dead.

He's thrown his bag across to the other side already, but what if the branch breaks before he makes it to the other side?

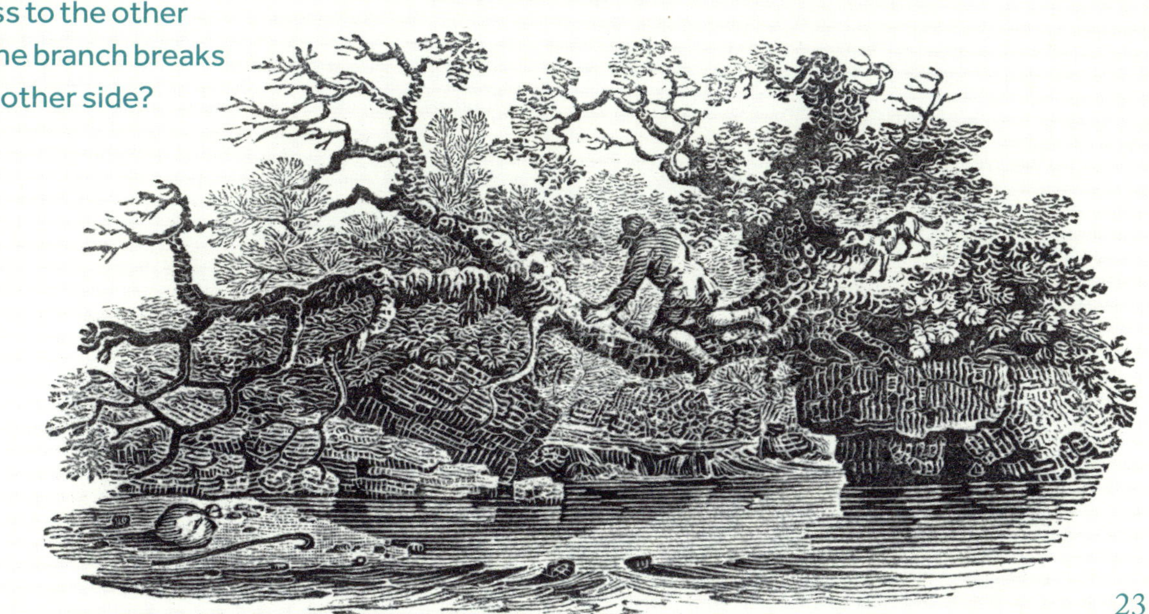

Bewick in business

In October 1774 Thomas Bewick's seven-year apprenticeship came to an end. He went home to Cherryburn.

In 1776 Bewick walked to Scotland and back, then travelled by sea to London. He was unhappy in the big city, so he returned to the North East.

For 20 years, Bewick worked in partnership with his former master Ralph Beilby, before eventually setting up on his own.

He took on a succession of apprentices, beginning with his brother John. Later he trained his own son Robert and several nephews but not his three daughters. Very few girls had the chance to learn a trade at this time.

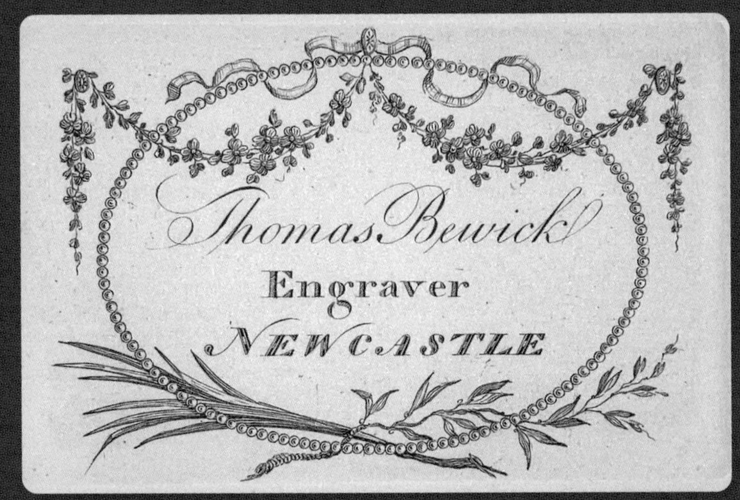

Newcastle was expanding rapidly. The coal trade, in particular, brought wealth, and commercial activity of all kinds followed. It was a good time to be an engraver because everybody seemed to want a fancy design to mark their property, sell their goods or promote their services.

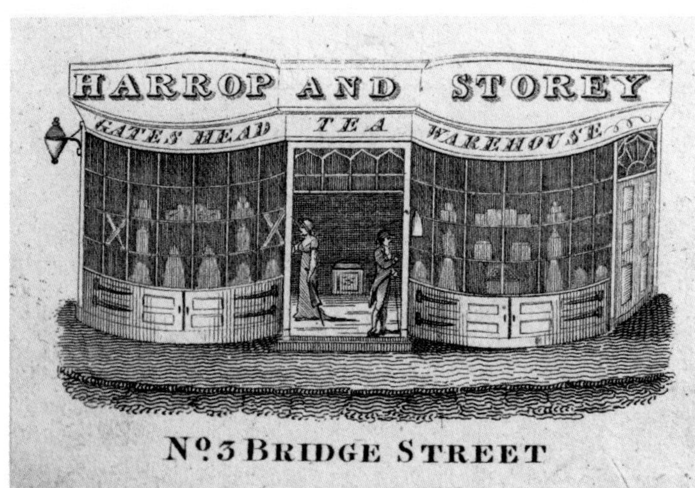

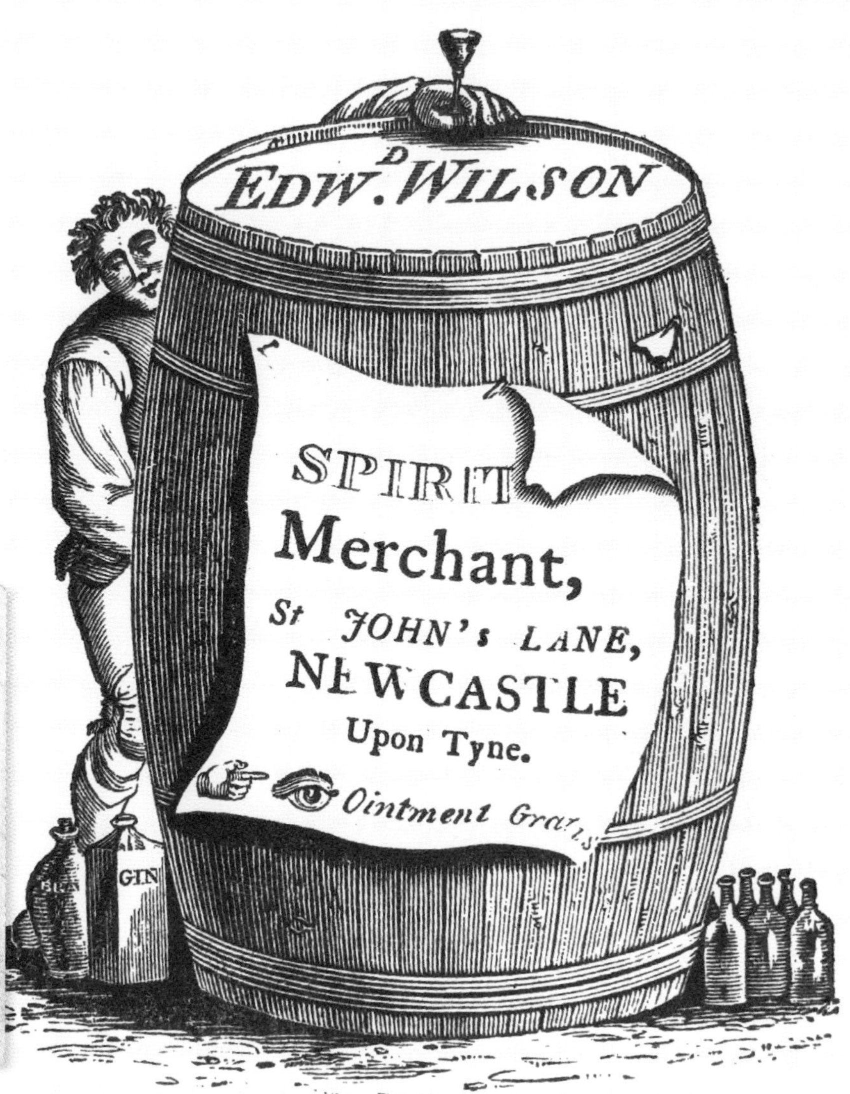

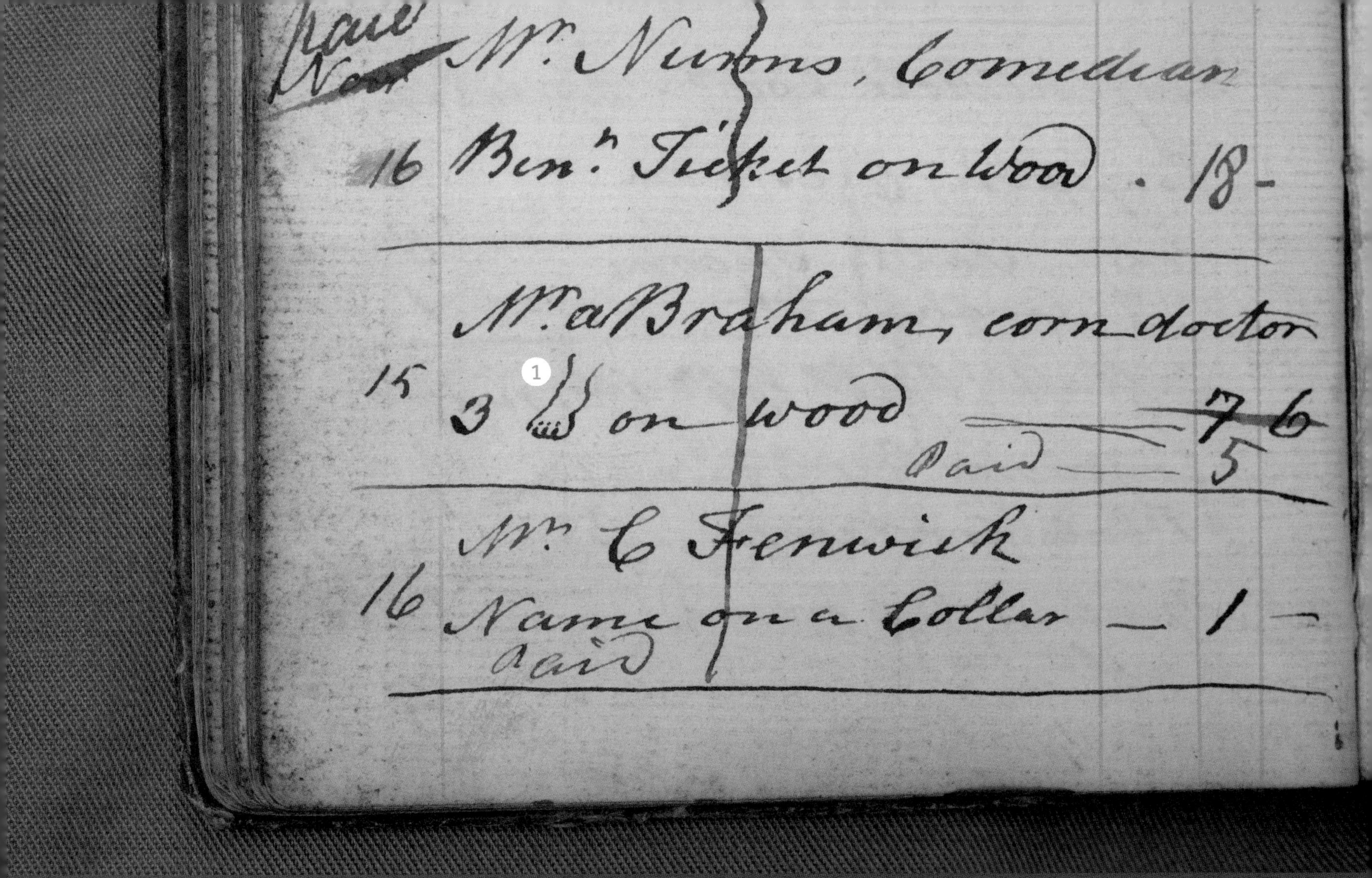

Mr. Nu..ns, Comedian
16 Ben.n Ticket on Wood . 18 -

Mr. A Braham, corn doctor
15 3 [foot] on wood ———— 7 6
                    Paid ———   5

Mr. C Fenwick
16 Name on a Collar — 1 —
    Paid

This picture shows an extract from Bewick's accounts for November 1793.

1 He has drawn a tiny foot next to the name of Mr Abraham, corn doctor. Mr Abraham had a bill of seven shillings and sixpence for an engraving on wood, but Bewick settled for five shillings. Perhaps he needed Mr Abraham to tend to his feet?

Keeping the books

In Thomas Bewick's busy workshop careful accounting was essential to the smooth running of the business. In his Day Books he recorded all the orders received and crossed them off when they were paid.

In another set of notebooks Bewick recorded all the money coming in and going out each week. Most clients settled their bills promptly and in full, but some had to be reminded.

Bewick's accounts show that J. Garnett the Chemist paid one pound and a shilling, on the nail, to have his business cards designed, engraved and printed.

Mr Garnett's shop was on the Quayside, so perhaps that is why he chose a riverbank image to advertise his business.

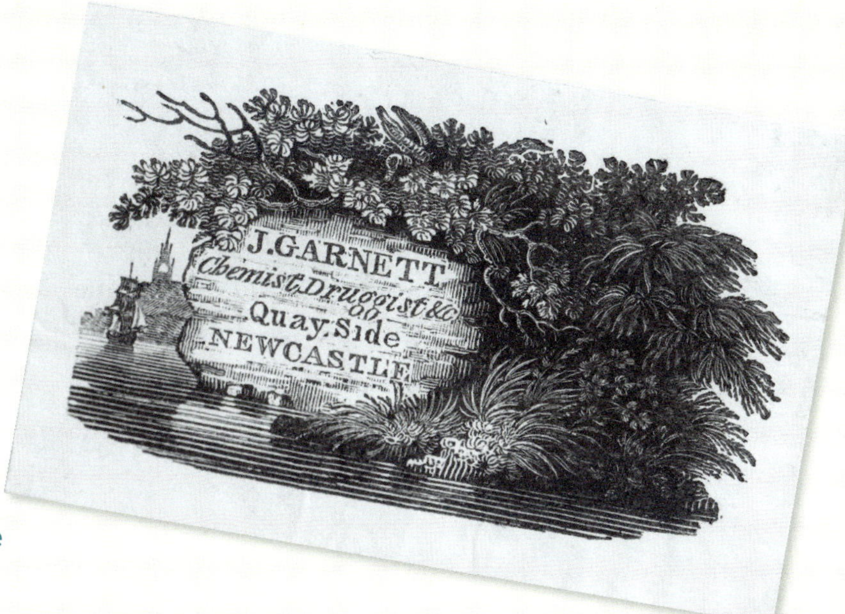

Away from the workshop

In Thomas Bewick's day there was plenty of entertainment in Newcastle: from horse racing on the Town Moor, to concerts and balls in the Assembly Rooms.

Mr Kinloch was a well-known local dancing master. Thomas Bewick's daughters went to his classes.

If it was raining, racegoers could do worse than visit Robertson's Umbrella Manufacturers on Newgate Street.

M.ʳ KINLOCH'S BALL. N.º

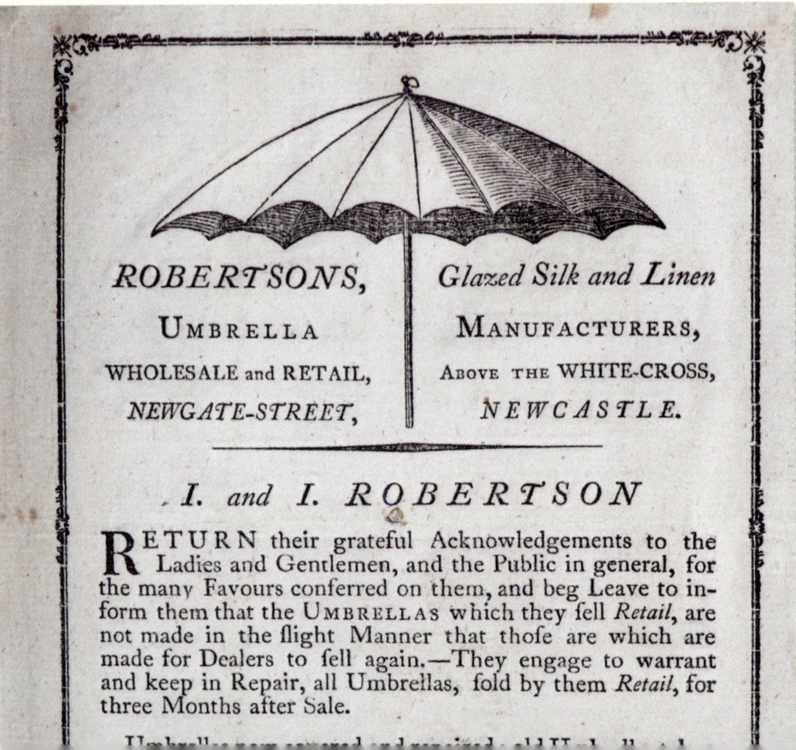

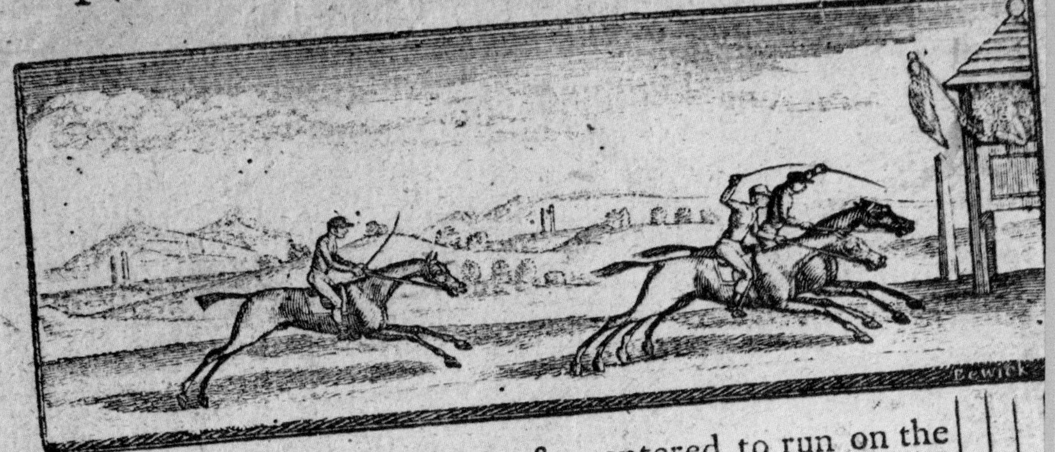

This handbill lists all the horses running in His Majesty's One Hundred Guineas race on 24 June 1782. Who do you suppose won?

Could it have been the Duke of Hamilton's bay horse, ridden by W. Hack in stripes?

Or perhaps Mr Fenwick's chestnut horse, **Anybody**, ridden by J. Cade in pink?

My money's on Mr Jolliff's horse **Foxhuntoribus**!

A tiger comes to town

In 1787 a magnificent tiger came to Newcastle as part of a travelling show. Thomas Bewick seized the opportunity to draw it. He had a close-up view and was able to capture all the subtle variations in the tiger's stripy coat.

From bristling whiskers to twitching tail,
Bewick's tiger ripples with fierce energy.

'The Tiger is the most rapacious and destructive of all carnivorous animals.'

The Tiger from *A General History of Quadrupeds*, 1790

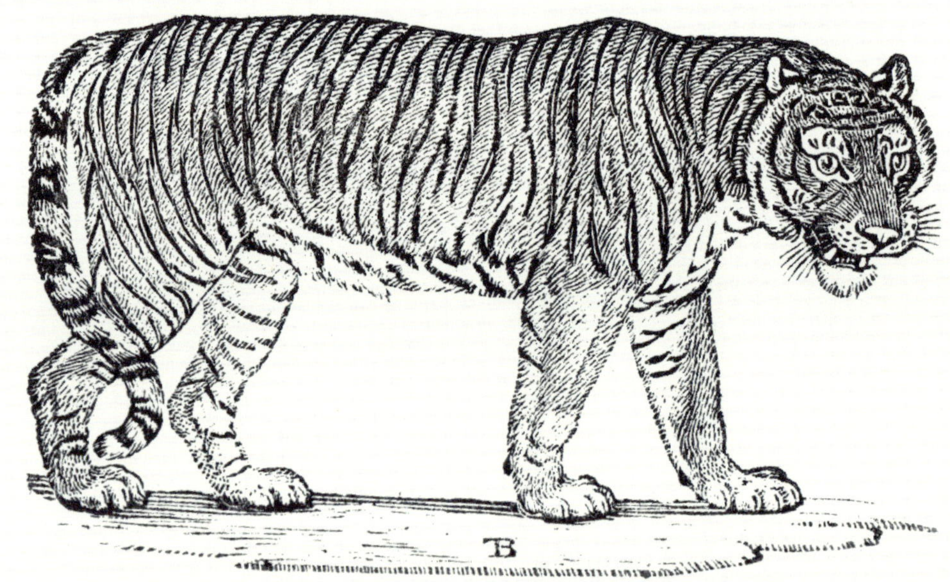

This large, coloured tiger print was specially created by Thomas Bewick
for Gilbert Pidcock, who owned a famous travelling menagerie.

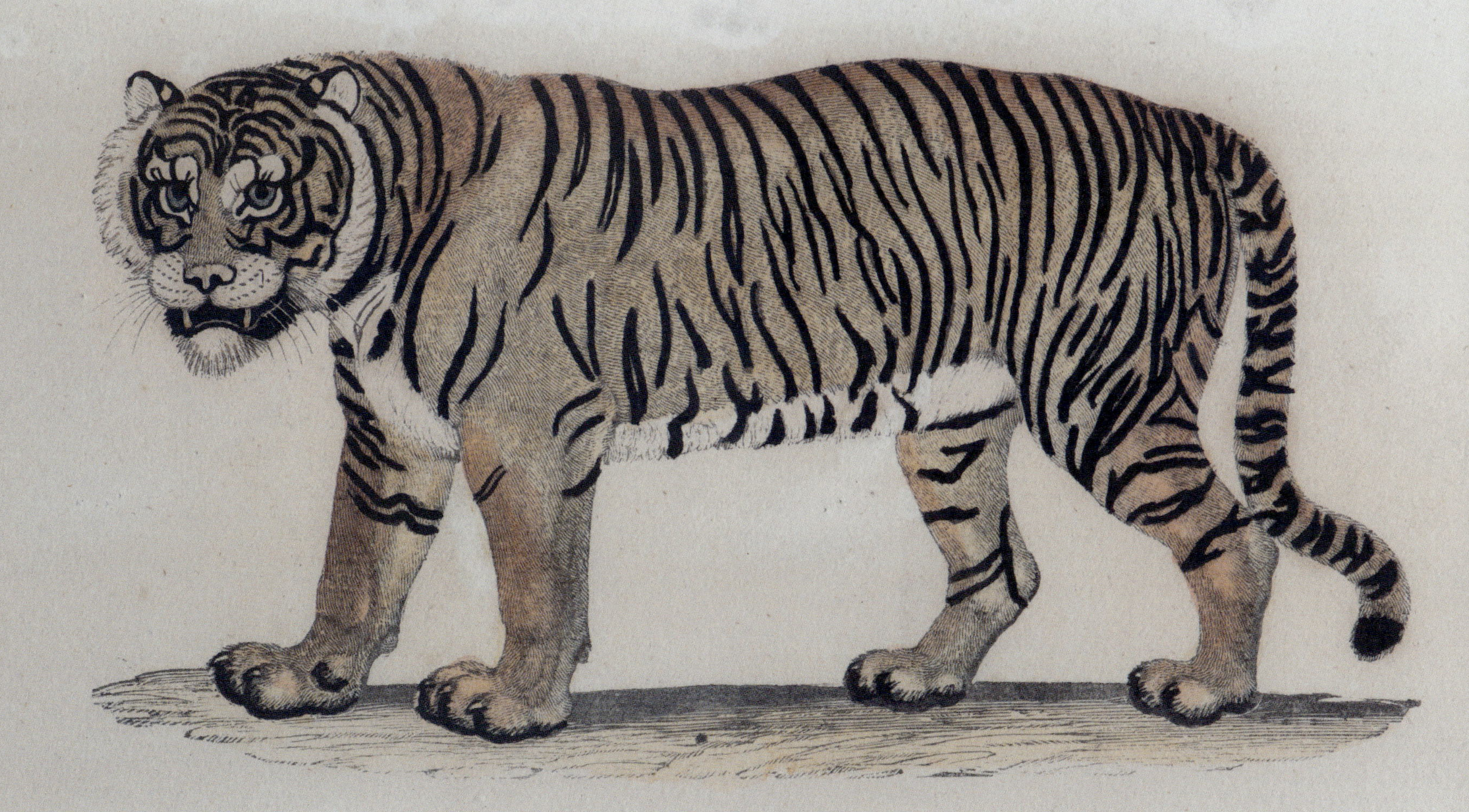

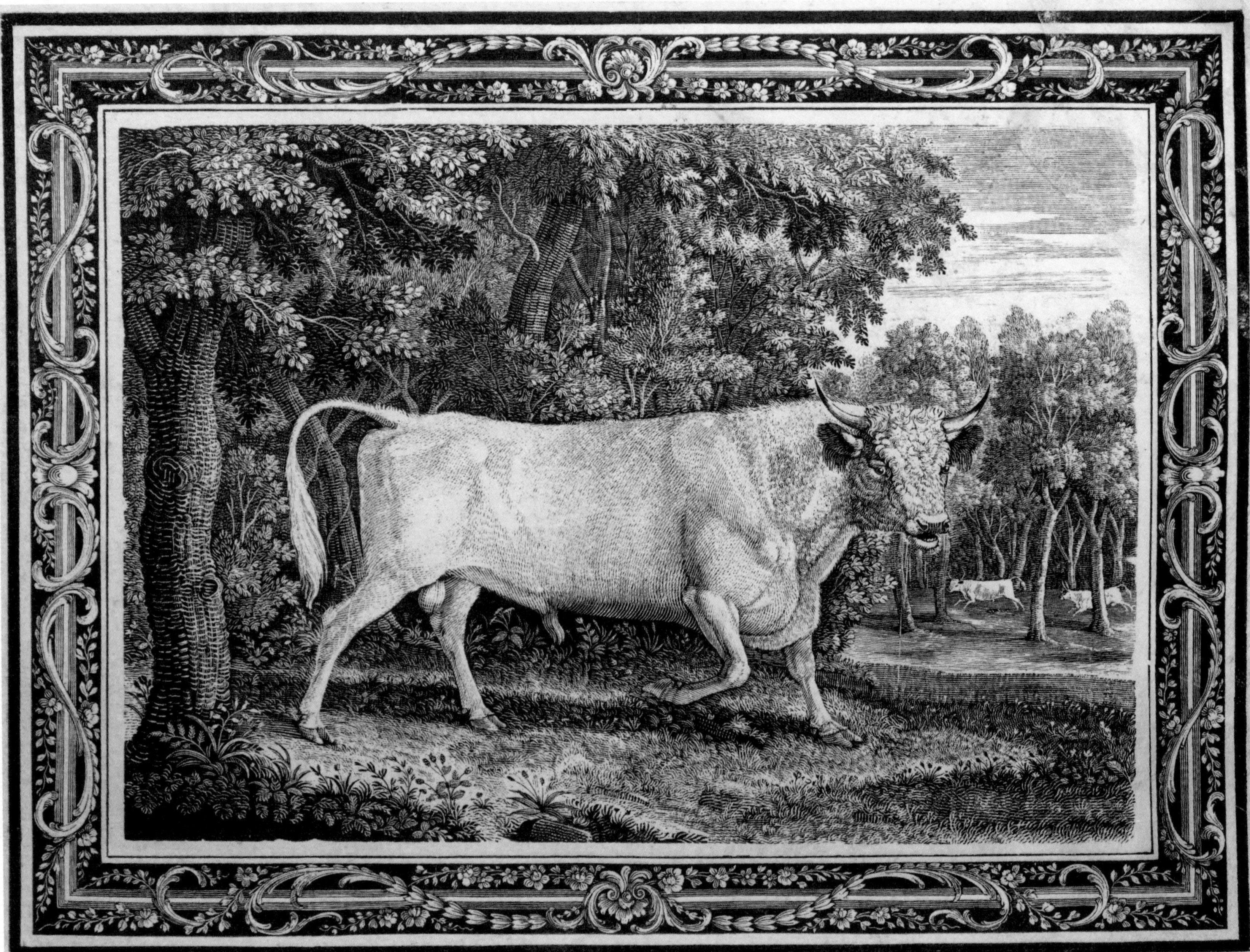

The Chillingham Bull

On Easter Sunday 1789 Thomas Bewick set off on foot to Chillingham in Northumberland, a distance of some 30 miles across country. He had been invited to draw the famous wild white cattle at Chillingham Castle.

Bewick wanted to draw the biggest bull in the herd, but it was much too lively, and he was forced to retreat to a safe distance. Instead, he drew a less mature beast, without a shaggy mane. Nevertheless, *The Chillingham Bull* became Bewick's best-known engraving.

'At the first appearance of any person they set off in full gallop, and, at the distance of two or three hundred yards, make a wheel round and come boldly up again.'

The Wild Cattle from *A General History of Quadrupeds*, 1790

Left: Thomas Bewick was commissioned to draw the wild cattle at Chillingham by Marmaduke Tunstall, of Wycliffe in North Yorkshire.

Thomas Bewick's Quadrupeds

By day, Thomas Bewick was busy with commercial work. In the evenings, working by candlelight, he could concentrate on his own projects. In 1790, *A General History of Quadrupeds* was published. The book included descriptions of 199 animals with illustrations by Bewick.

A quadruped is an unfamiliar name for a creature with four feet!

Thomas Bewick loved drawing animals. His pictures are exquisitely detailed and full of character. He used the tiniest marks to build texture – can you see how he has distinguished between the rough coat of the lumpy camel and the glossy flank of the horse?

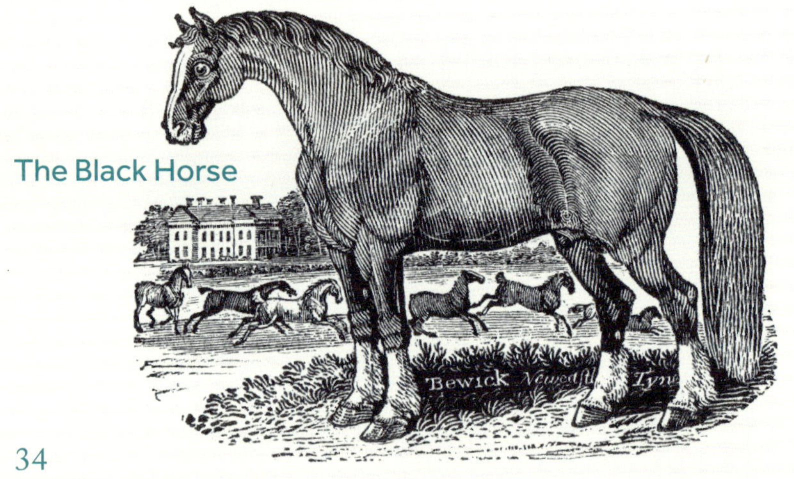

The Black Horse

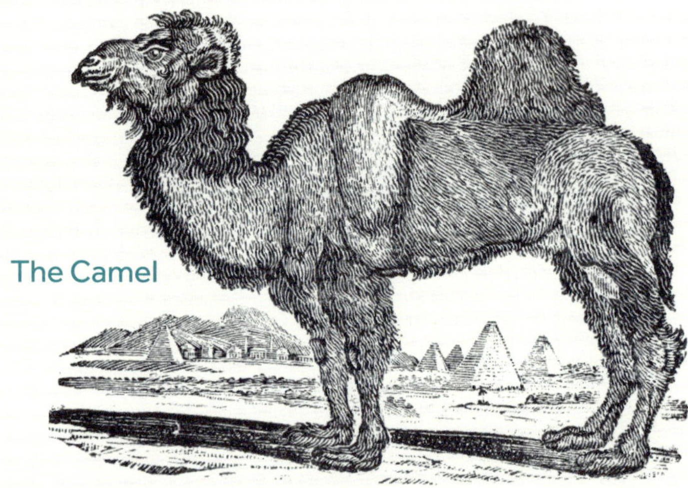

The Camel

'Tale-pieces'

In gaps at the end of sections Bewick inserted extra pictures which he called 'tale-pieces' because each one told a story in miniature. Most of these bore no relation to the text but they added considerably to the enjoyment of the book.

Quadrupeds was a huge success. Within a year, a second edition was published, 'with many Additions and Improvements.'

This 'tale-piece' illustration of a man pole-vaulting across the river is from Bewick's *Quadrupeds.* It comes at the end of the section about the 'Oran-Outang'.

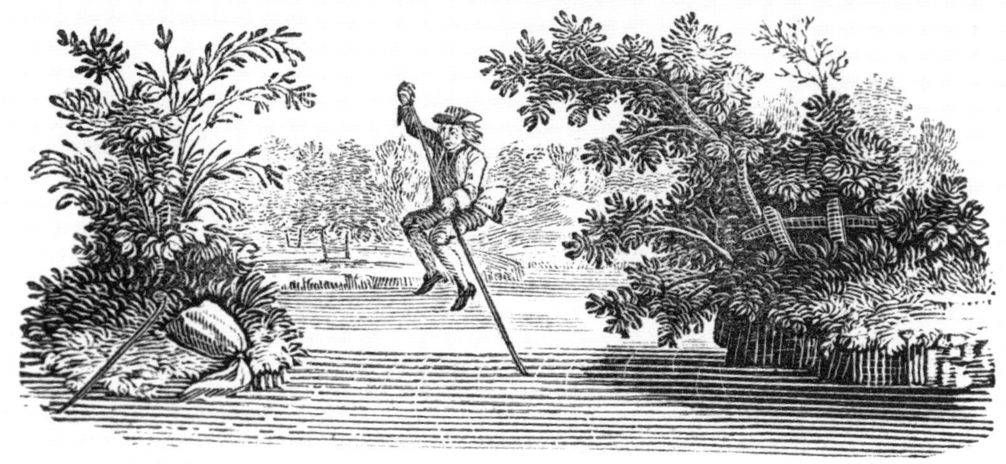

Bewick's Birds

Of all the books illustrated by Thomas Bewick, the most famous is his *History of British Birds*.

The book was published in two parts: *Land Birds* in 1797 and *Water Birds* in 1804. Each part contains detailed descriptions and illustrations of over 100 birds.

Bewick consulted bird books by other authors, but wherever possible he drew on his own careful observations. He depicted each bird in its natural habitat, which makes the drawings more lifelike and adds interest for the reader.

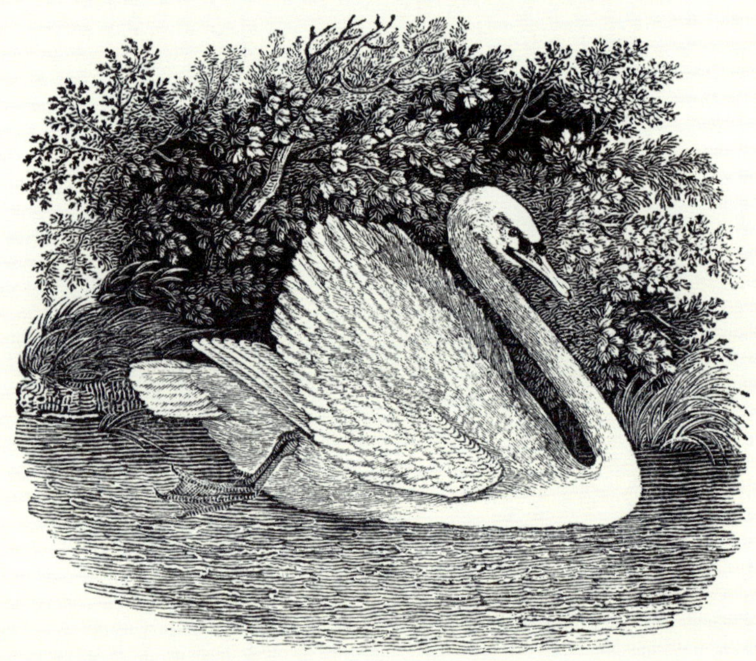

'the pure resplendent whiteness of the majestic Swan.'

The Mute Swan from *Water Birds*, 1804

'This busy little bird is seen frequently in our gardens and orchards, where its operations are much dreaded by the over-anxious gardener.'

The Bluetitmouse from *Land Birds,* 1797

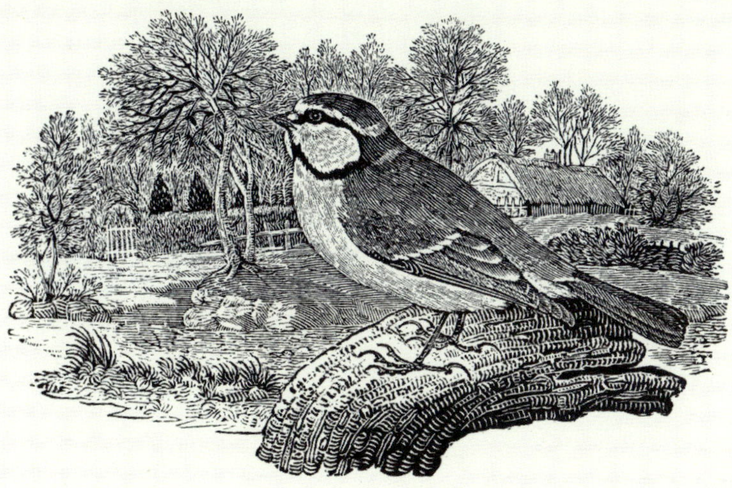

Could this beady-eyed blue tit have been a bird that Bewick saw in his own garden?

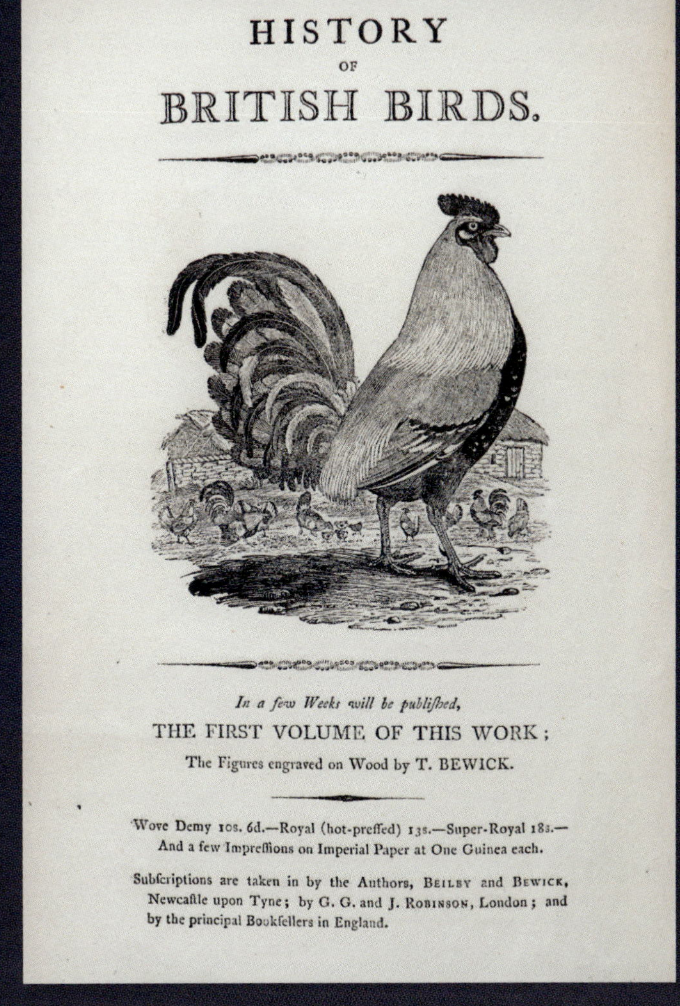

This is an advertisement for the first volume of *British Birds*. Bewick has chosen this splendid illustration of a cockerel to announce the new publication.

The heron

Thomas Bewick knew about herons. He would see them standing in the River Tyne, or flying overhead, with their huge wings flapping.

This bird with its long legs, knobbly knees and sharp-clawed feet is well-adapted to standing on the muddy shores of the river watching for fish.

Its feathers, flat and oily, keep the bird dry and warm in all weathers.

The heron has caught a wriggling eel but can't swallow it without first opening its long beak… what if the eel just manages to escape? Will it quickly disappear into the river or will the bird snatch it back and – snap – swallow it whole?

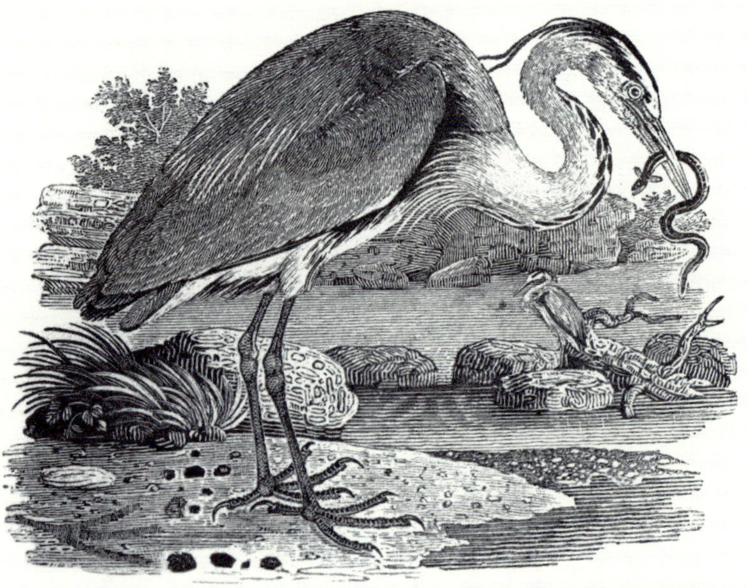

'Although the Heron is of a long, lank, awkward shape, yet its plumage gives it, on the whole, an agreeable appearance.'

The Heron from *Water Birds,* 1804

The corncrake

In summer, when the grass was high in the fields around Cherryburn, Thomas Bewick often heard the "crex crex" cry of the corncrake. Yet the bird was seldom seen. It ran nimbly through the thick grass, camouflaged.

How did Thomas Bewick manage to draw this elusive creature in such detail? Here's the secret: someone caught a live corncrake and sent it to Bewick's workshop, where he was able to observe it close at hand.

Nowadays, there are no corncrakes in Northumberland, but if you travel to the Western Isles in summer, you might still be lucky enough to hear their "crex crex" cry.

'Its well-known cry is first heard as soon as the grass becomes long enough to shelter it, and continues till the grass is cut.'

The Corncrake, from *Land Birds*, 1797

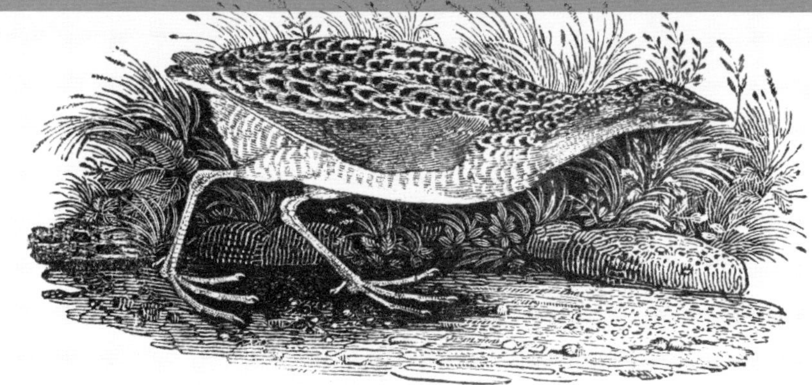

Miss Carr, Mr Bewick and the puffin

Harriet Carr was an accomplished artist who lived near Gateshead. She was keen for Thomas Bewick to take a look at her paintings.

Miss Carr had another thing to show him: a stuffed seabird. She didn't know its name, but she thought that Mr Bewick might like to draw it for his book of water birds.

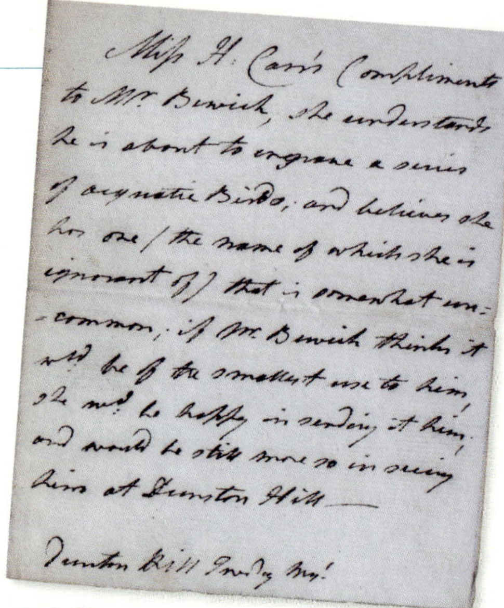

Letter from Harriet Carr to Thomas Bewick.

'Miss H. Carr's compliments to Mr Bewick. She understands he is about to engrave a series of aquatic Birds, and believes she has one (the name of which she is ignorant of) that is somewhat un-common. If Mr Bewick thinks it would be of the smallest use to him, she would be happy in sending it him, and would be still more so in seeing him at Dunston Hill.'

The mysterious bird turned out to be a puffin! How strange that Harriet Carr, who had travelled widely across Europe, was not familiar with this colourful visitor to the Northumberland coast.

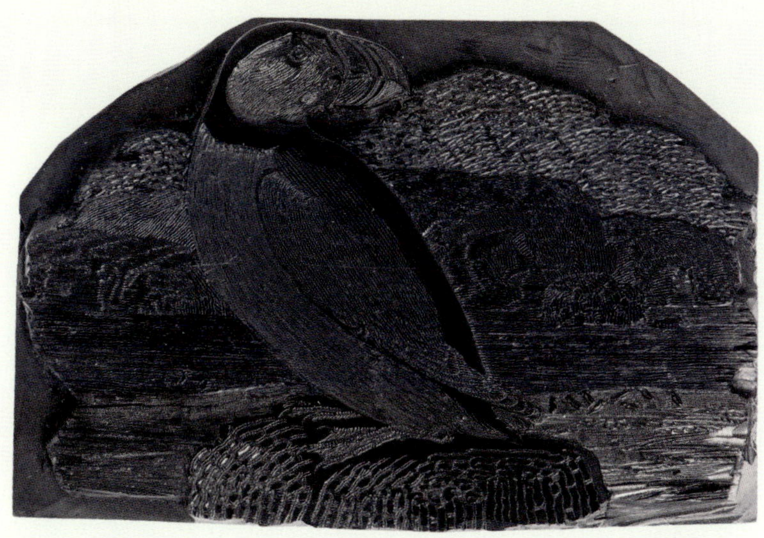

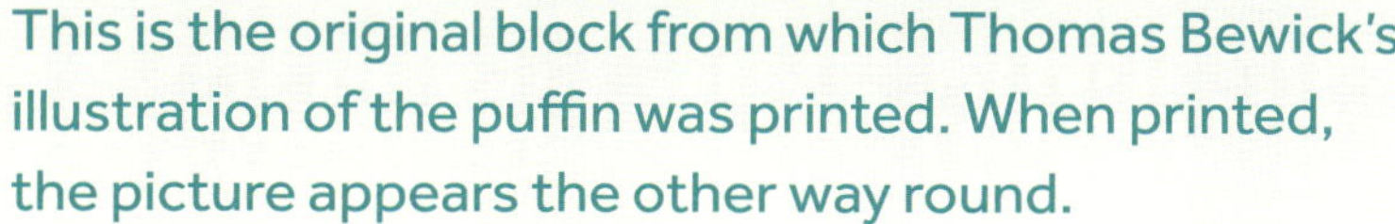

This is the original block from which Thomas Bewick's illustration of the puffin was printed. When printed, the picture appears the other way round.

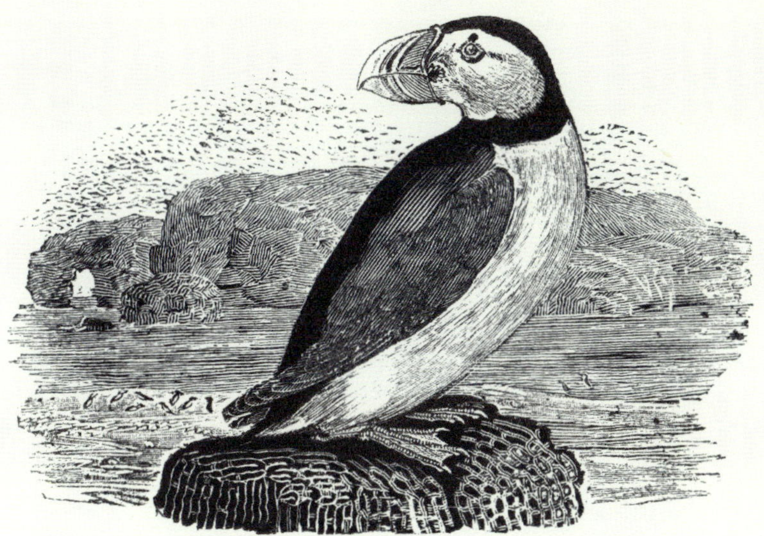

Thomas Bewick and the Fables of Aesop

Thomas Bewick was especially fond of the ancient Fables of Aesop. He loved these pithy moral stories with talking animal characters. Bewick was a man of strong opinions and believed that fables were a good way of teaching young people to behave well.

In 1818, when he was 65 years old, Bewick fulfilled a long-held ambition by publishing his own version of Aesop's Fables. Bewick's Aesop included 165 stories, each with its own illustration.

His son Robert and two of his apprentices helped with the engraving.

This is Bewick's illustration for one of the best-known fables: *The Hare and the Tortoise.*

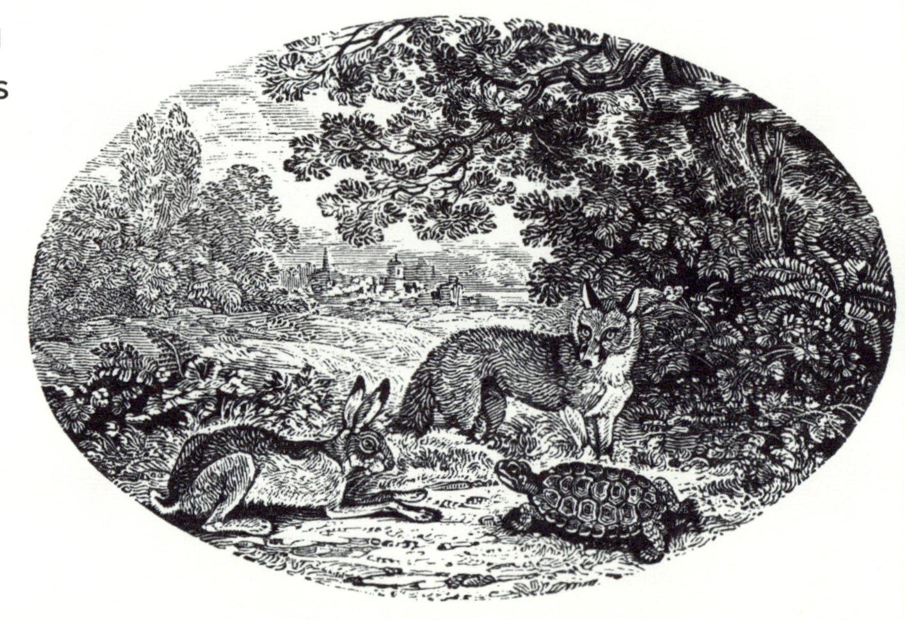

The Crow and the Pitcher

The moral of this ancient fable is that what cannot be achieved by strength may yet be attained by ingenuity.

One day, a very thirsty crow discovered a pitcher (a tall jug) with water in the bottom, out of reach. The clever bird picked up pebbles from the ground and dropped them, one by one, into the pitcher. As the pitcher filled with pebbles, the water rose to the brim and at last the crow was able to drink his fill.

The story about the clever crow is universal but in Bewick's illustration the setting looks like rural Northumberland.

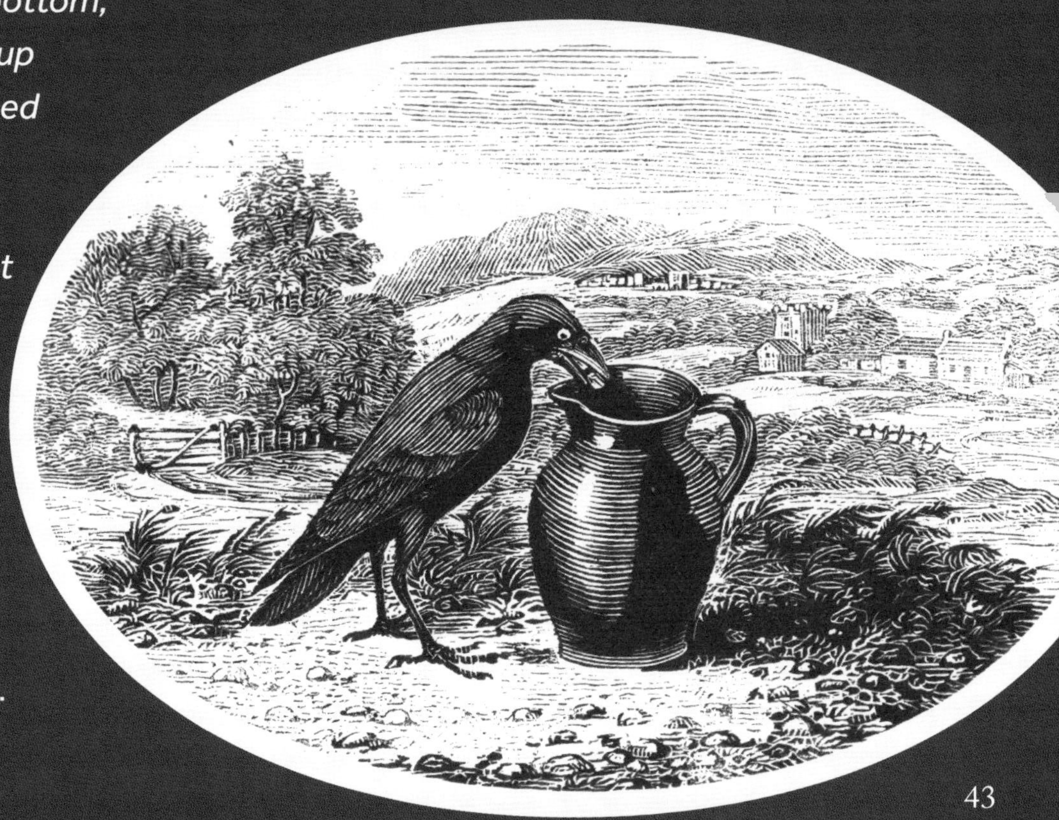

A life well lived

Thomas Bewick continued drawing and engraving into his seventies. He published new editions of his earlier books, wrote his *Memoir,* and, together with his son Robert, started work on a *History of British Fishes*. He never stopped having ideas for new pictures.

In November 1828, after a short illness, Bewick died. He was 75 years old. He was buried next to his wife Isabella in the churchyard at Ovingham, across the river from his childhood home at Cherryburn.

His son Robert was a gifted engraver, but his real passion was playing the Northumbrian Pipes. The book of fishes was never published.

A

HISTORY

OF

BRITISH FISHES.

THE FIGURES ENGRAVED ON WOOD,

BY T. BEWICK & SON.

This Work is intended to be put to Press in 1826,

AND TO BE

PRINTED ON IMPERIAL, ROYAL, AND DEMY PAPERS,

TO MATCH THE HISTORIES OF QUADRUPEDS, AND BRITISH BIRDS,
AND THE FABLES OF ÆSOP.

None of Thomas Bewick's four children married, so there are no direct descendants. Bewick's elder daughters Jane and Isabella lived to a grand old age and were proud guardians of their father's artistic legacy.

The art of wood engraving gradually fell out of fashion, but admirers of Bewick's work formed collections of his books, prints and engraved blocks. Many of these are now in public libraries and museums, where they can be seen and enjoyed by everyone.

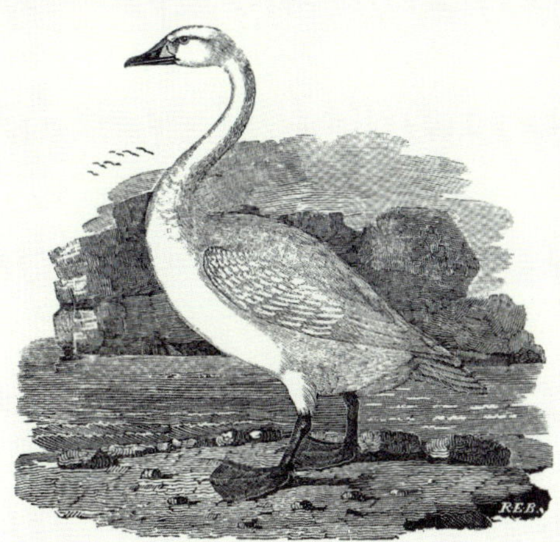

When a new species of Swan was discovered in Northumberland in 1830, it was named 'Bewick's Swan'. This illustration of the bird was made by Robert Bewick for the 1847 edition of *Water Birds*.

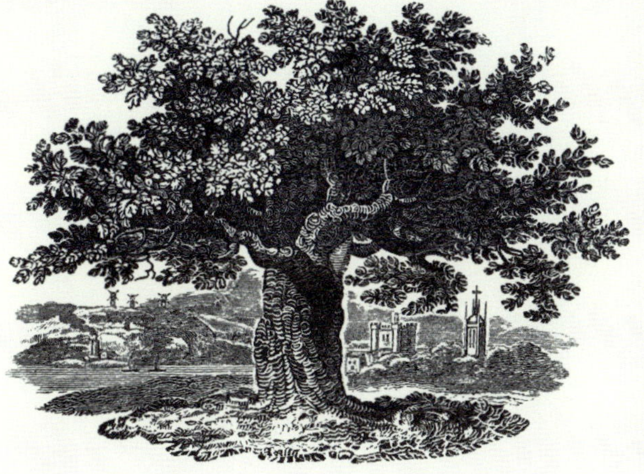

This illustration of an old oak tree with the townscape of Newcastle in the background was chosen by Newcastle Public Library as the bookplate for their Bewick collection.

Find out more

Most of the Bewick images in this book are taken from the Pease Collection at Newcastle City Library – a treasure trove of Bewick books, engraved blocks, drawings, correspondence and printed ephemera. The collection also includes Thomas Bewick's original toolbox. These are not on public display but can be viewed by prior arrangement – contact information@newcastle.gov.uk

The website of The Bewick Society (www.bewicksociety.org) is a mine of information about Thomas Bewick's life and work, and other Bewick places and collections. Membership of the Society includes free entry to Cherryburn and a programme of interesting talks and events.

There are many books about Thomas Bewick's life and work. *Nature's Engraver* (2006) by Jenny Uglow is a good place to start.

'Tale-piece' illustration from *Water Birds*, 1804

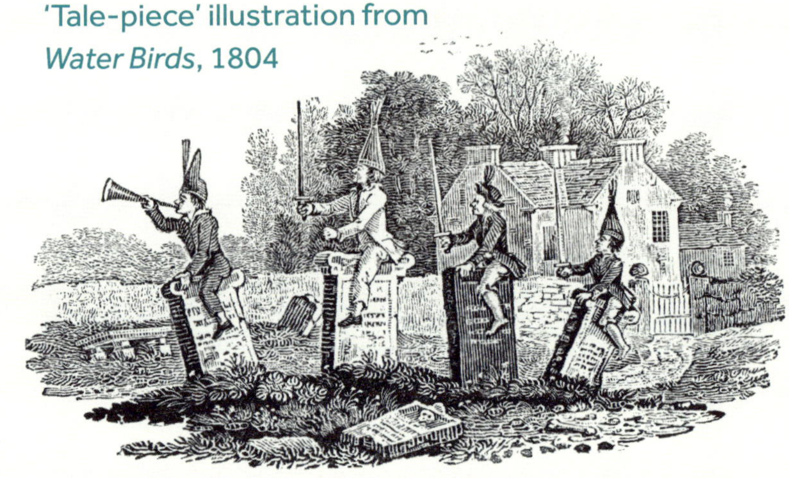

Bewick places to visit

The birthplace of Thomas Bewick at Cherryburn is managed by the National Trust. It is a lovely tranquil place to visit in spring or summer. On display are copies of Bewick's books and some of his engraved blocks; there is also a printing workshop with occasional demonstrations and a cottage garden. Opening times are limited so check the National Trust website before planning a visit.

In Newcastle, a blue plaque marks the site of Thomas Bewick's workshop at Amen Corner behind St Nicholas's Cathedral. Another plaque on Bewick Street, across the road from Central Station, marks the location where he lived for much of his adult life. Head to the Laing Art Gallery to see Nicholson's portrait of Thomas Bewick and a display of his books and prints.

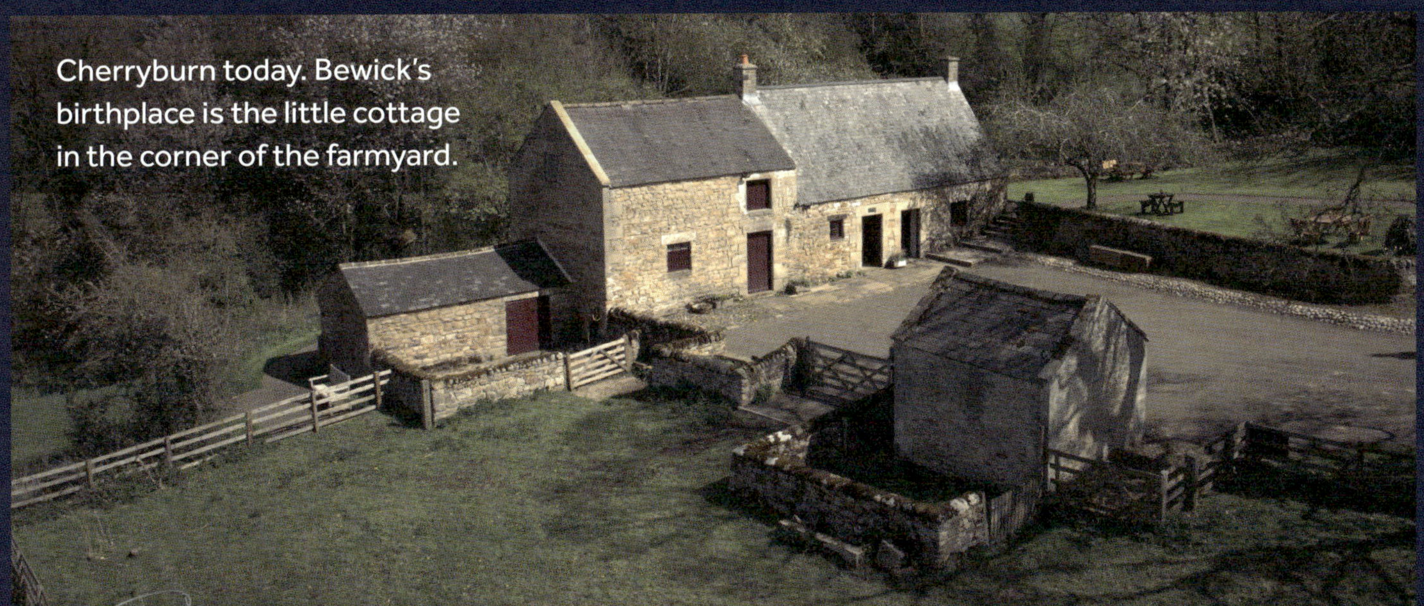

About Open Ended Books

Open Ended Books is a dementia-friendly publishing initiative from creative ageing charity Equal Arts. *Bewick Tales* is our first publication. Our aim is to create beautiful and life-affirming books that stimulate imagination and creativity and help maintain positive relationships between people living with early to moderate dementia and their family and friends.

We combine words and images to create stories that are both easy to follow and rich with intriguing details that provoke curiosity and conversation. Every aspect of the text and layout is informed by the needs of our readers and we welcome your feedback.

To find out more please scan this QR code or go to
www.equalarts.org.uk/open-ended-books

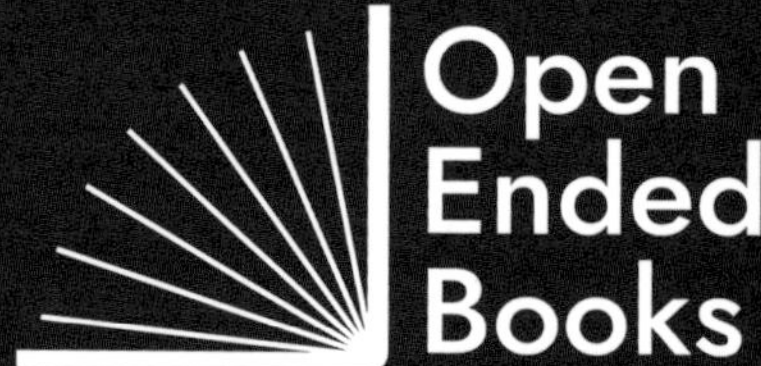

About Equal Arts

Equal Arts is a leading creative ageing charity supporting older people and those living with dementia.

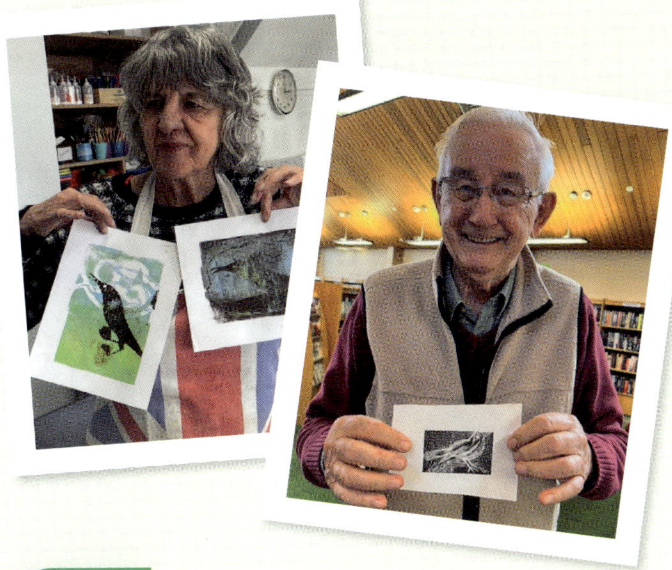

equal arts

Improving older people's lives through creativity

Our programmes provide artist-led creative opportunities to improve wellbeing and reduce loneliness. We work across artforms with visual artists, musicians, theatre practitioners, writers and curators providing opportunities for people to explore their imagination and live in the moment.

About the author

Sarah Lawrance is a curator and writer based in Newcastle upon Tyne. She loves working with collections and people to create stories and is proud to be collaborating with Equal Arts on the development of Open Ended Books.

Acknowledgements

Equal Arts is grateful to the many people and organisations that have generously contributed time and expertise to the development of this book. We are especially grateful to Newcastle City Library, the Bewick Society and the National Trust at Cherryburn for their support and to our book designer Wendy Lewis for her painstaking work. Thank you also to Chris Daunt, wood engraver and block maker, for allowing us to photograph him at his studio, just a few miles from where Thomas Bewick lived and worked.

Above all we would like to thank those people living with dementia who have shared their insights with us; their feedback has helped to make this a better book and establish our new imprint, Open Ended Books.

Sarah Lawrance would like to thank David Foster, Dr. Julia Green, Ceinwen Haydon, Robert Lawrance and Dr. Marie Leahy for their advice and encouragement.

This publication has been made possible with funding from Innovate UK: DCMS Create Growth Fund and the National Lottery Heritage Fund.

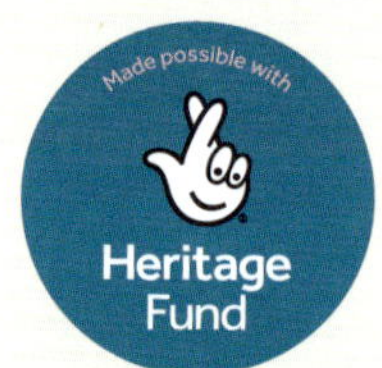

Picture credits

Except where otherwise stated, the pictures in this book are reproduced from items in the Pease collection at Newcastle City Library. Photography by Colin Davison.

Page 5: William Nicholson's portrait of Thomas Bewick – reproduced by permission of the Laing Art Gallery.

Page 9: Robert Bewick's drawing of the sitting room at Cherryburn belongs to the National History Society of Northumbria and is reproduced by permission.

Page 13: extract from Ralph Beilby's weekly engraving account book, TWA 1269/34, reproduced by permission of Tyne and Wear Archives.

Page 14–19: photography by Colin Davison.

Page 26: extract from Messrs Beilby and Bewick workshop day book, TWA 1269/14, reproduced by permission of Tyne and Wear Archives.

Page 40: the letter from Harriet Carr to Thomas Bewick belongs to the Wordsworth Trust in Grasmere and is reproduced by permission.

Page 47: aerial view of Cherryburn – photograph by Alex Harrison, reproduced by permission of the National Trust.

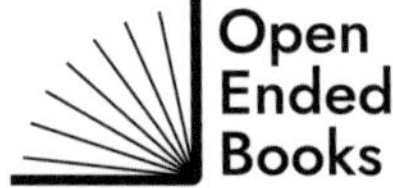

Published by Open Ended Books, 2024

Copyright Equal Arts, 2024

Open Ended Books is the publishing imprint of Equal Arts.

Equal Arts is a registered charity no. 517352.

Postal address:
Equal Arts,
Newcastle City Library,
33 New Bridge Street,
Newcastle upon Tyne NE1 8AX

Website:
www.equalarts.org.uk/open-ended-books

Author: Sarah Lawrance

Foreword: Peter Quinn

Design: Wendy Lewis

The moral rights of Sarah Lawrance to be identified as the author of this work has been asserted in accordance with the Copyright, Designs and Patents Act 1988.

ISBN 978-1-7385229-0-3

A CIP catalogue record for this book is available from the British Library.

Printing arranged by Biddles in association with Carbon Neutral Climate Partner manufacturers.

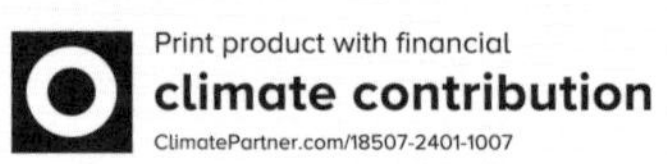

Produced using FSC and PEFC certified materials.

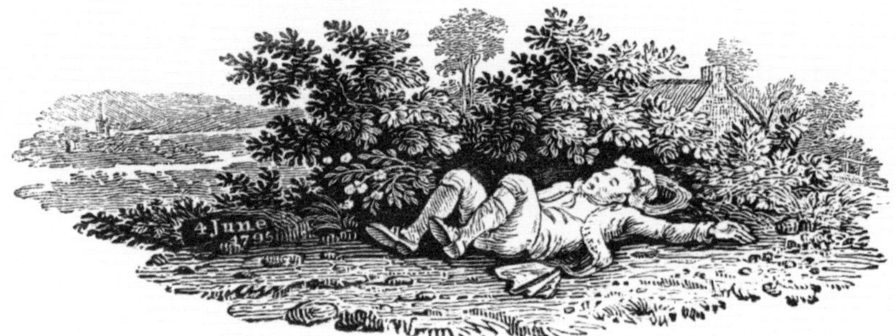

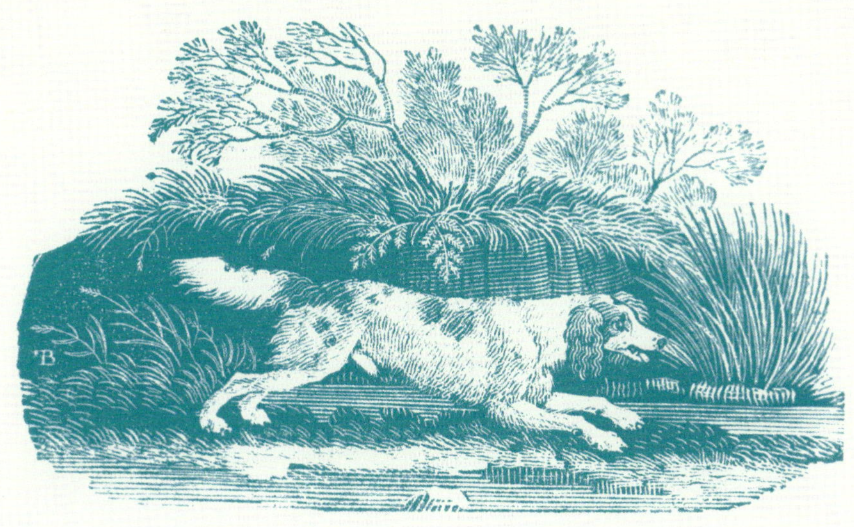

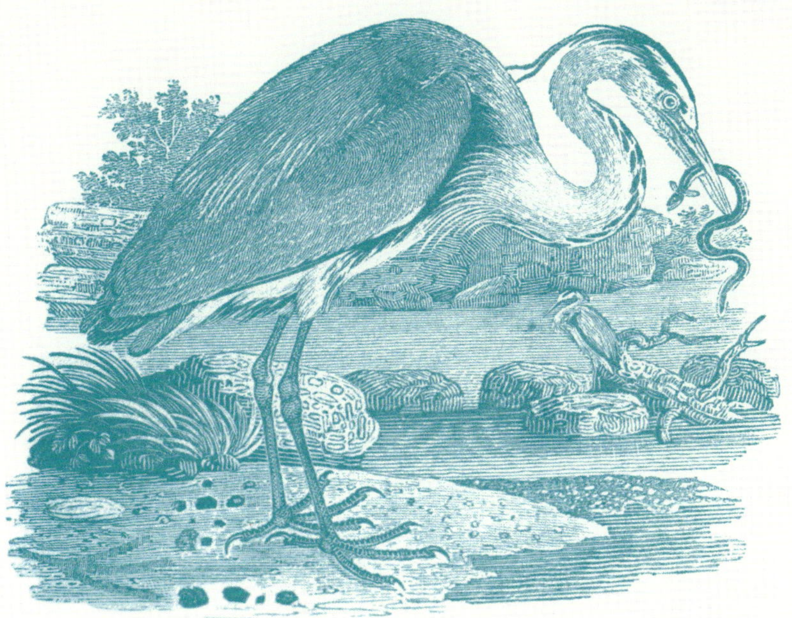

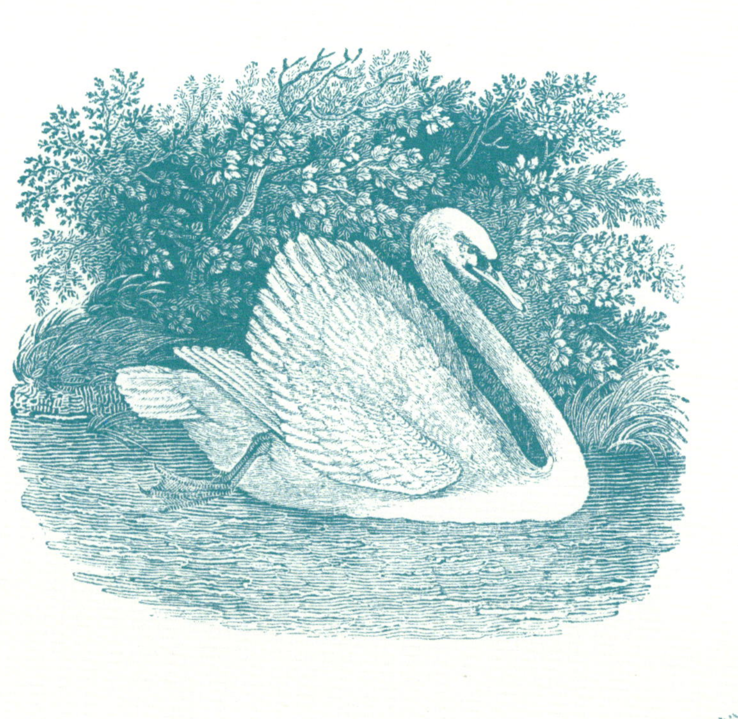

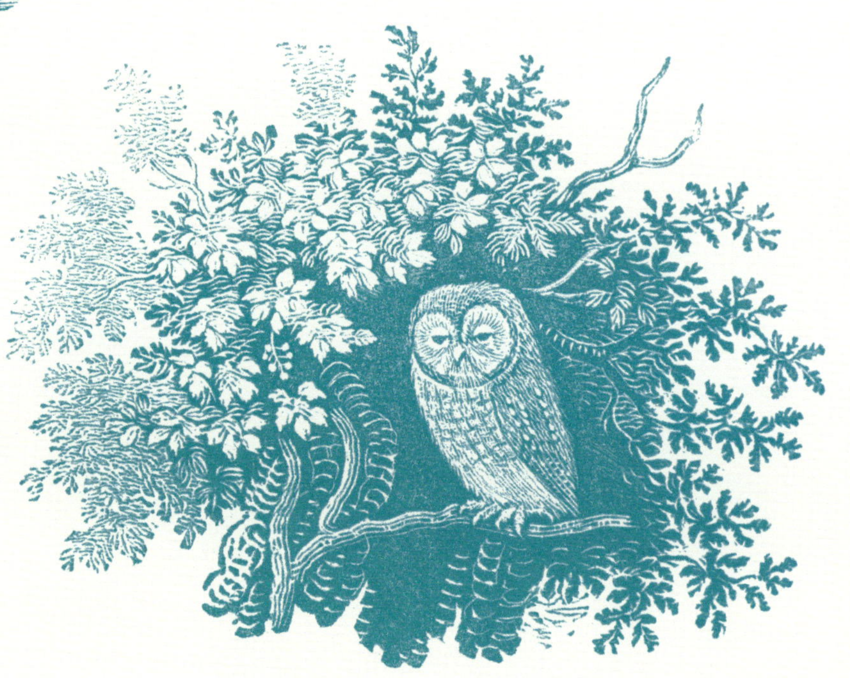